STYLE:

Acting
in
High
Comedy

THE APPLAUSE ACTING SERIES

General Editor: Maria Aitken

STYLE:

Acting in High Comedy

MARIA AITKEN

NEW YORK • LONDON

An Applause Original
STYLE: ACTING IN HIGH COMEDY
By Maria Aitken

Library of Congress Cataloging-In-Publication Data
Aitken, Maria.
    Style : acting in high comedy / Maria Aitken.
        p.   cm. -- (The Applause acting series)
    "An Applause original"--Verso t.p.
    Includes bibliographical references.
    ISBN 1-55783-214-5 (trade pb)
    1. Acting. 2. Comedy. 3. English drama (Comedy)--History and criticism. 4. Manners and custom in literature. I. Title.
II. Series.
PN2071.C57A38 1996
792'.028--dc20   96-31292
                                                    CIP

British Library Catalog in Publication Data
A catalogue record for this book is available from the British Library

APPLAUSE BOOKS   A&C BLACK

211 West 71st Street   Howard Road, Eaton Socon
New York, NY 10023   Huntington, Cambs PE19 3EZ
Phone (212) 496-7511   Phone 0171-242 0946
Fax: (212) 721-2856   Fax 0171-831 8478

Distributed in the U.K. and the European Union by A&C Black

Printed in Canada

TABLE OF CONTENTS

Acknowledgments

My thanks to
Michael Kahn and
Earle Gister and to
my students at Juilliard and Yale drama schools

1

WHAT IS HIGH COMEDY?

High comedy is an addiction. It's heady stuff to be able to use language like a rapier, to be in temporary possession of wit, elegance, precision. It's often suggested that only particular types with particular gifts can play high comedy, but good playwrights strive to leave clear signposts, to make the essence of their play actor-proof, so why should we be so modest or so vain as to think a play cannot accommodate us? The alchemy is almost all in the text. Few plays reward mere diligence so richly: the shape and the sound of the speech is part of its meaning; in this regard, form *is* content. The plays respond to any actor who learns to allow the language to lead the way.

High comedy is not a dead genre; although it covers plays ranging from Congreve to Coward it would also include recent work by John Guare, Christopher Durang, Nicky Silver, and Harry Kondoleon, among others. Sometimes high comedy is known as comedy of manners, an expression which goes some way towards a definition because it makes explicit the fact that the manners—the social rules—of the play are essential to its identity. We do comedies of manners no service by judging them without understanding their period. We have to participate in the playwright's world without surreptitiously investing it with ideas that were not in his mind at the time. In other words, we have to succumb to the rules of the society he invents plus his own moral position; the *style* of this particular play.

What are the other essential ingredients of high comedy? First, as I've indicated, *language* is used as a weapon and as a tool for seduction. With this high level of verbal sophistication comes wit—the pickling agent that has preserved the ideas in plays written three hundred years ago and kept them fresh in the repertoire. Second, a *society*. The characters who populate high comedy are not, as is often supposed, immensely grand, but they are usually of a leisured class. These are people with enough time on their hands to develop and enjoy their verbal skills. The leading characters often flout the conventions, rejecting the manners which get rewarded in their particular world. Third, a quality of *paradox*. High comedies are not bloodless, refined, wordy plays—their themes are sex, money, and social advancement. They contain a splendid contradiction: wit and elegance at the service of man's basest drives. The whole reason that high comedy has proved such a durable form is that it reveals the truth about human nature, warts and all, but does so with glorious pyrotechnics of language and behaviour. It uses society's most sophisticated social accomplishments, intellect and wit, to mock society itself; the glitter reveals the grubbiness.

This book isn't a critical examination of high comedy. Rather, it's a collection of suggestions for the middlemen: the actors who have to catch the comic spark from the playwright and pass it on to the audience. The effort involved must be imperceptible: one has to acquire the cleverness, the articulacy, the febrility of the characters—and then make the whole laborious exercise seem like swimming through silk. Acting styles date horribly, but making it look easy was as much a prerequisite in the seventeenth, eighteenth, and nineteenth centuries as it is now.

High comedy is associated with dangerous and misunderstood words that make the modern actor fear phoniness and bombast: "delivery," "wit," and "style." *Delivery* implies a barrier of vocal mannerism between the speaker and the play. But in high comedy the words demand display as well as truthfulness. It's not old-fashioned bravura to capitulate to the relish for speech that the characters possess: it's the main means of getting close to the core of the play.

Wit, another disabling word for actors, will never take care of itself unless your brain and your tongue are in harness. Too often those witty phrases fall like pennies into mud because you have not made your character's thought process your own thought process. And you must familiarize yourself with verbal games like repartee, which involves an idea passing from one speaker to another, often echoing key words, and irony, where language is used as a cover up: a decoy to the true intention. These forms of wit will be analyzed in more detail later, but the key to them all is comprehension and delight. The characters in high comedies don't, after all, find verbal sophistication difficult or unfamiliar; they enjoy it as you might enjoy slang. To embrace the pleasure and ease of wit is to go a great way towards acquiring it.

The *society* is a combination of the period and the unique world of the play, making an entirely new reality which nods at history but does not recreate it. An author does not describe his age, he distils it for his own ends. Similarly, the actor researches the period, trawling for clues that relate to his character's predicament in a play. Read contemporary diaries, go to portrait galleries, photographic archives, magazine libraries. The distinction between public and private behaviour is a powerful clue to the prejudices of a particular period, so try to get hold of unpublished letters and diaries, family photo albums, anything that reveals the unguarded self. Occasionally, period seems to create a psychological gap between us and the character. So look for the constants first—the capacity to love, hate, feel jealousy, be tired, bored and so on—that connect us to the people of earlier times. Then remember that the differences between us and the world of the play are part of what compose the style—moral values, customs, language.

Sometimes, however, we are too burdened with fact to process it into invention; sometimes we still persist in looking through a modern prism. Much as I value all forms of exploration, I would hate it to be at the expense of the gusto and commitment that is so essential to high comedy, so if you can't find reality in a period play, I offer you a suggestion from Uta Hagen's *Respect for Acting*. She advises actors to stop worrying about the academic research side of it and seek instead the sensation of taking a vacation, the absence of responsibility, the interest in one's appearance, the search for self-gratification.

While I'm on the subject of period, I'll touch on "period movement," although I've deliberately avoided it in the rest of the book. I've never really understood what the term means. Movement is dictated by actualities: by your clothes, or by the need to avoid sitting next to your enemy, or to establish your position in the pecking order. By all means, look up in a book such as Lyn Oxenford's *Playing Period Plays* the way to bow or curtsey in the manner appropriate to the period, but then make the convention serve you, not the other way round. We have all endured those Jane Austen-type films where a ball scene is suddenly populated by guests straight out of dancing academy. If your character is a vain old woman with stiff knee joints, she would have found an idiosyncratic method of curtseying that would not betray her—drawing attention to her top half with a flourish, while barely bobbing, perhaps—and never mind that everyone else sinks to the floor. It's vital that you dominate your clothes, too—they are intended to express your character's personality, not to dictate it. Inhabit your costume with utter familiarity, and make it work for you; after all, your character chose it in order to convey an image to the world. Always try to talk to the designer at an early stage, because your collusion will make it much easier for you to take complete, authoritative possession of the final outfits. In rehearsal, mock up an approximation of your costume as soon as you can. Sneakers are *never* any help, unless your character will be wearing them in performance. You must have the right sort of shoes or the right length skirt early in the process. The impact of costume on movement very soon becomes apparent—the circle of a train in motion has to be respected by all; a sword can trip you up; long lace cuffs predispose flamboyant hand movements. The creative part occurs when clothes and accessories become an extension of the wearer, part of your sexual armoury, your arsenal of flirtation, of dominance, of submission. After all, that's how someone of the period would have used them.

Handling of props provokes consideration of period, because objects take on different potencies in different eras. Because it's not appropriate now to put on a lot of make-up in public, we might consider a character wielding lipstick and compact at a restaurant table to be bad-mannered or provocative. But from the 1920s right through the 1950s it was socially acceptable to repair make-up in public. Indeed, the fashion of bright lips and a matte skin required constant repair, and moment-to-moment checks were necessary. Similarly, once skirts became short enough to reveal seamed stockings, then that odd backwards twist, the checking of straight seams, became a female reflex. It was not a come-on, though of course, like any gesture, it could be made provocative when desired. And what about the cigarette, deprived of its old erotic potential in our modern, "No Smoking" world? It was Edith Evans who said, "Do everything with a fan except fan yourself with it"; props are not useful for their function, but for what they tell us about the character's state of mind. There is a thesis to be written about Bette Davis's manipulation of the cigarette. Evelyn Waugh recaptures a lost world when he describes the "batsqueak of sensuality" set up by the transfer of a cigarette from a man's lips to a woman's. If you hear the batsqueak, your audience will hear it. That's the kind of period movement worth having.

When you're searching for your character you look for what makes that character different from everyone else, for their distinguishing characteristics. Finding out what is comedic about your character is no less a process of selection, but it is something that actors in pursuit of total identification with their roles are reluctant to admit to. Characterisation does, however, require a certain detachment: you must both *know* what it is that makes you funny and *forget* what it is that makes you funny. In other words, you need to be sufficiently detached from your character to draw him a little out of proportion. Then, and only then, can you "go in," as it were, and acknowledge with approval the small distortions you've created in him. And your approval of the distortions must be high enough that they seem to you to be an integral part of a very harmonious whole! The character of Faulkland in Sheridan's *The Rivals* is a good example. Early in rehearsal an actor playing Faulkland must see this character's flaw of jealousy with detachment, and be able to acknowledge poor Faulkland's ridiculous lack of balance. Then, having established the necessary degree of excess, he must progress to perceiving that same jealousy as logical, balanced behaviour. Some actors tread this tightrope instinctively. It's all made considerably easier if you have sympathy with the flaw in question because, to some degree, you share it!

Method actors may be made rather uneasy by this view, but one can't afford the luxury of "possession by character" in high comedy. The capacity to step back and see if it works is the greatest protection we have against self-indulgence. Connection and concentration aren't broken in any fundamental ways by a moment's detachment to check our excesses or lack of clarity. It's simply examining the same instant from another angle. As actors, we constantly experiment with the ability to exist on more than one level, and I've always thought that the sort of fleeting separation of mind and body that some acting demands resembles descriptions of near-death experiences. This is a lofty comparison, but the fact that we use the same equipment for living that we do for pretending is what makes acting so oddly demanding. The same arms that hold our lover in life hold our lover onstage. We weep from the same tear ducts, smile with the same lips. As with the patient who suddenly looks down at himself on the operating table while the drama of resuscitation is in full swing, and then just as sud-

denly joins his body again, so do we actors experience simultane-
ous connection and disconnection with our character. Comedy requires a parallel universe.

But a parallel universe does not preclude a desire to live only
in the moment in performance. In fact, I have come to the conclusion that the real art of performance lies in doing all the work
you possibly can in preparation, then having the courage to forget
it. It feels as if there is a creature in my brain called "Anticipation,"
and only by concentration and relaxation can I keep that creature
dormant. Any failure of concentration, any self-consciousness, and
the spectre of "What happens next?" crowds into my mind. I
loathe the sense of estrangement which follows. I like long runs
because they give me time to rout anticipation. When concentration and relaxation work together, it feels as if the play is an un-
scheduled event, even though there is, of course, no other route
through the evening except that laid down by the text. I stand in
the wings not knowing when I will step on the stage, trusting there
will be a reason to do so. I meet other characters as if for the first
time, hear what they say as if for the first time.

I didn't go to drama school. I acquired the little I know by
making mistakes in public. Existing in the moment, I have con-
cluded, is only possible when we have trained our physical and
mental responses at a deep level in rehearsal, because then we are
free. There are rare cases when we are instinctively in tune with
the character we play, but, for the most part, we find our way by
dogged hard work.

2

DELIVERY:
Naturalism and
Energy

NATURALISM

Do naturalism and high comedy seem odd bed-fellows? Together they create a heightened reality. If you adopt the relish for language which is common to all the plays, then the naturalistic way to perform them is not by obscuring the verbal skill but by delighting in it. The text is like a map, full of signs that must not be ignored. You can't override them in the service of some idea of modern naturalism, you must subject yourself to the form first of all, *then* make it as natural as you can. This approach will reward you, for as you pick up the "habits" contained in a good text, by degrees they will bring your character to life. The structure of the sentence impels your voice to the right inflection. You will be animated by the relationship between a particular language and the reality you already possess.

Actors persist in believing that they do not exist outside a role, that they bring nothing to lines by speaking them until they have discovered a character. In high comedy that is putting the cart before the horse. The feel of the words spoken aloud leads us towards discovery. Words have an uncanny alchemy, and by merely speaking them as if we thought of them (which is easier said than done) we assimilate their meaning to an extent that allows us to feel real. Actor, character, and language combine to make their own reality. That's what any actor wants, and we have all experienced those miserable draughty moments when our psychology is incomplete. Sometimes it's the writer's fault; more often it is ours. Always start with the words, for they can lead you most of the way. In his *Essay on Comedy*, Meredith wrote of Congreve's Millamant in *The Way of the World*: "It is a piece of genius in a writer to make a woman's manner of speech portray her. You feel sensible of her presence in every line of her speaking."

The first step is to understand every nuance of dialogue. This may mean not only paraphrasing the play in detail (not the gist, but the exact sense of every sentence), but also looking up the meaning of any puzzling words in an etymological dictionary such as the twelve-volume *Oxford English Dictionary*. Words can frequently change their meaning from one period to another, so you must make sure of the author's intention. Good editions of plays will have comprehensive notes to help you out. If you are having trouble making the text sound spontaneous because the language is unfamiliar to you, use your paraphrase to catch your spontaneous *modern* inflections. Listen to yourself as you express the ideas in colloquial language. You may find an intonation that will help you get the meaning across when you revert to the more complicated language. Repeat the speech over and over again until it poses no problems of pronunciation, rhythm, breathing—the meaning will sing out loud and clear. It is then your property. You are in charge of it, not the other way round. You are still quite free to change your interpretation, but the *form* of expression is no barrier to whatever you choose to do. Pretty soon you will feel that those words are the only possible means of expressing yourself and they will no longer seem difficult and archaic. Most importantly, the audience will understand your speeches, because when your tongue and your brain operate in harness they can overcome the occasional obscure piece of text and *communicate*.

A slow brain and the resulting slow tongue not only injure the text, they imply your character is not securely himself or herself and deflate the bubble that is high comedy. The audience doesn't have to understand every single word to grasp the sense, but you do. Without you acting as an authoritative transmitter of the playwright's intentions, the audience doesn't have a hope of comprehending. Pace can sometimes make a complex speech easier for an audience's collective ear to grasp, but pace is not to be confused with speed. You cannot speak more quickly than you form the thoughts. Pace only occurs if you are in charge of the ideas at every moment. Speed up your brain and tongue in tandem.

I know I am breaking an ancient taboo when I say this, but never mind: you can't begin to act until you know your lines. The more reflexive they become, the more power you have over them. It's absolute nonsense to claim that by learning them you get stuck with an early interpretation and can't change it. The real problem is that one has no flexibility when one is flailing around trying to remember lines. My advice coincides with Noel Coward's—come to rehearsal knowing every word, then you can use the time productively. Actors have abetted a conspiracy of laziness by finding imaginary drawbacks to arriving word perfect. If you want to achieve naturalism, a total command of the text is the only route—and learning the lines is the easiest part of the whole discipline.

✧ ✧ ✧

PRACTICING NATURALISM

Let's look at the wooing scene between Mirabell and Millamant from William Congreve's *The Way of the World*. This is a Restoration comedy written in the seventeenth century and we have to make it accessible not only to our tongues and brains but to an audience's collective understanding. The play has a labyrinthine plot which I don't propose to outline here—suffice it to say that Mirabell and Millamant are the vital young moderns who give us hope for the future by displacing a decadent social order represented by all the other characters. In the playing, the many-layered story is perfectly comprehensible, though, and a lesson never to underestimate an audience's I.Q. Something extraordinary can happen to a group of mixed intelligence as they sit there in the dark. They concentrate, their emotions become available, and their collective intelligence is about 25 percent higher than a simple calculation of the average. They *want* to understand.

On the surface, Mirabell and Millamant are complete opposites. Mirabell exudes solemnity ("that violent and inflexible wise face, like Solomon at the dividing of the child in an old tapestry hanging") and demands "plain-dealing and sincerity." Millamant has an airy vitality that leaves him gaping: "Think of you! To think of a whirlwind, though 'twere in a whirlwind, were a case of more steady contemplation." And her language is often extraordinarily modern. An actor friend of mine who has played Mirabell told me gloomily, "Of course Millamant has a hot line to the audience—her stuff is so much easier to understand." It's true that Mirabell's speeches are sometimes grammatically complex—there's one in this scene that's a devil—but they must be tamed until they trot off the tongue. We are aiming to defeat the twin curses of period drama—stiffness and incomprehensibility—and to bring the whole thing alive.

As is frequently the case in seventeenth- and eighteenth-century plays, the names furnish clues. Millamant means "a thousand loves." The word "lover" did not mean someone with whom she had a sexual relationship, but simply an admirer. Virginity before marriage was a social imperative. However, adultery afterwards was perfectly fine, provided it was discreet:

> **MILLAMANT:** Beauty the lover's gift! Lord, what is a lover, that it can give? Why, one makes lovers as fast as one pleases, and they live as long as one pleases, and they die as soon as one pleases; and then, if one pleases, one makes more.

Mirabell (*admire belle*, "he admires beauty" in French, or perhaps *mirabilis*, "wonderful" in Latin) loves Millamant. But we are not sure of her feelings until the end of the scene I have chosen from Act IV. They are obviously a promising combination, but Millamant has been avoiding Mirabell on the issue of marriage:

> **MIRABELL:** I would beg a little private audience too—you had the tyranny to deny me last night, though you knew I came to impart a secret to you that concerned my love.

Let us assume this scene is the first time they have been alone together. Unless we know otherwise, it seems a daft choice to put them in a situation familiar to them, when we could be experimenting with fresh, surprised responses. It is an extremely erotic situation, brimming with sexual tension. Mirabell, after all, is uncertain of the outcome. The man pursues and the woman resists—that is the form. But there is nothing anaemically formal about their exchanges, because there are powerful feelings beneath. Her coquetry may hide the truth (it's not until he's left the room that she can say "I find I love him violently") but their desire for each other is in every thrust and parry of their exchanges. The scene, as you will see, is nevertheless full of surprises that spring from Millamant's caprice and individuality; Mirabell's radical ideas about how a wife should behave; his grasp of Millament's nature; and, of course, their dazzling wit. It's a wonderful example of the working-out of a pre-nuptial contract between highly unconventional people, as they put aside their illusions about marriage and recognise their responsibilities to each other.

When I work on this scene with a group of actors, I try to surprise them into a spontaneity of inflection, particularly if they are nervous of the language. I ask them to start the scene with the line "Do you lock youself up from me to make my search more curious?" Then I send Mirabell out of the room. While he is gone I ask Millamant to hide herself. Then I tell Mirabell he can come in. Sometimes he has started speaking before he realises Millamant has eluded him, and has to stop and find her before he can proceed, by which time his voice has acquired exactly the right combination of enchantment and exasperation. Sometimes he enters expecting trouble, so his relief and delight at finding her are palpable. In all cases, an actual search impels his voice to the right inflection. Then I ask Mirabell to stalk Millamant in and out of an obstacle course of chairs—not boisterously, but with both of them aware of every move and potential move—while they say the first few speeches. It gives a sense of pursuit and an intense awareness of the other's physical presence. Sometimes, to boost their capacity to use the language to flirt, I give each actor one end of a long silk scarf as an embodiment of the erotic thread between them. A little tug for initiating an erotic moment, a little

---

THE WAY OF THE WORLD
BY WILLIAM CONGREVE
Act IV, Scene 1

MILLAMANT: Ay, ay; ha, ha, ha!
Like Phoebus sung the no less amorous boy.

[*Enter* MIRABELL.]

MIRABELL: *Like Daphne she as lovely and as coy.* Do you lock yourself up from me, to make my search more curious? Or is this pretty artifice contrived to signify that here the chase must end and my pursuit be crowned, for you can fly no further?

MILLAMANT: Vanity! No—I'll fly and be followed to the last mo-

(*Scene continued on p. 20*)

tug for responding. The action filters straight through to the voice. Sometimes I play some *presto* spinet music by C. P. Bach, or something delicate and quirky by Satie. They don't dance to it, but it affects their movement, liberating them from All Those Words.

But the very first step is to make sure you understand every word, so that there is no skating over uncertain moments. Here is a paraphrase of the scene. I stress that it's just *a* paraphrase, because there is always room for debate.

THE WAY OF THE WORLD
Act IV, Scene 1
PARAPHRASE

MILLAMANT: [*First line of a couplet by the poet Waller.*]

MIRABELL: [*Second line*] Are you hiding to make my search more interesting? Or is this charming trick designed to show me my hunt shall be rewarded, now that I have caught up with you, because you can't run away any more?

MILLAMANT: What a vain notion! I shall always be pursued to

(Paraphrase continued on p. 21)

(Scene continued from p. 18)

ment. Though I am upon the very verge of matrimony, I expect you should solicit me as much as if I were wavering at the grate of a monastery, with one foot over the threshold. I'll be solicited to the very last, nay, and afterwards.

MIRABELL: What, after the last?

MILLAMANT: Oh, I should think I was poor and had nothing to bestow, if I were reduced to an inglorious ease and freed from the agreeable fatigues of solicitation.

MIRABELL: But do not you know that when favours are conferred upon instant and tedious solicitation, that they diminish in their value, and that both the giver loses the grace, and the receiver lessens his pleasure?

MILLAMANT: It may be in things of common application, but never sure in love. Oh, I hate a lover that can dare to think he draws a moment's air independent on the bounty of his mistress. There is not so impudent a thing in nature as the saucy look of an assured man, confident of success. The pedantic arrogance of a very husband has not so pragmatical an air. Ah! I'll never marry, unless I am first made sure of my will and pleasure.

MIRABELL: Would you have 'em both before marriage? Or will you be contented with the first now, and stay for the other till after grace?

MILLAMANT: Ah, don't be impertinent! My dear liberty, shall I leave thee? My, faithful solitude, my darling contemplation, must I bid you then adieu? Ay-h adieu, my morning thoughts, agreeable wakings, indolent slumbers, all ye *douceurs*, ye *sommeils du matin* adieu. I can't do it, 'tis more than impossible. Positively, Mirabell, I'll lie a-bed in a morning as long as I please.

(Scene continued on p. 22)

(Paraphrase continued from p. 19)

the very end. Even if I were going to marry you, I would expect you to pursue me as urgently as if I had practically decided to enter a convent, my foot over the threshold. I am the sort who must be chased to the bitter end, and even after that.

MIRABELL: What, even after marriage and bed?

MILLAMANT: I'd feel worthless if my life became dull and I was spared the delightful exhaustion of listening to men begging for my attention.

MIRABELL: But when you grant a favor after a lot of trivial and boring begging for it, it's not worth much. The person granting the favor loses face, and the person receiving it has less pleasure.

MILLAMANT: That might be true about ordinary matters, but not where love is concerned. I can't stand a man who thinks he can so much as breathe in without his girlfriend's permission. There's nothing more annoying in the world than a cocky-looking chap, who thinks he's going to get his way. Even the smug look of a husband isn't as annoyingly conceited as that. Oh, I'm never going to get married unless I'm absolutely sure of having my own way and my own enjoyment.

MIRABELL: Do you want both those things before marriage? Or would you be happy to have your way now, and wait for the enjoyment until after the ceremony?

MILLAMANT: Don't be cheeky! Must I give up my freedom? Have I got to say good-bye to solitude and time to ponder? Oh, oh, farewell to private thoughts in bed in the morning, to waking up slowly and delightfully, to dozing lazily, all those sweet things, those dreamy mornings—no, I can't give them up, it's out of the question. Mirabell, I'm definitely going to lie in bed in the morning as late as I want.

(Paraphrase continued on p. 23)

(Scene continued from p. 20)

MIRABELL: Then I'll get up in a morning as early as I please.

MILLAMANT: Ah! Idle creature, get up when you will—and d'ye hear, I won't be called names after I'm married; positively I won't be called names.

MIRABELL: Names!

MILLAMANT: Ay, as wife, spouse, my dear, joy, jewel, love, sweetheart and the rest of that nauseous cant in which men and their wives are so fulsomely familiar; I shall never bear that. Good Mirabell, don't let us be familiar or fond, nor kiss before folks, like my Lady Fadler and Sir Francis; nor go to Hyde Park together the first Sunday in a new chariot, to provoke eyes and whispers, and then never to be seen there together again, as if we were proud of one another the first week, and ashamed of one another for ever after. Let us never visit together, nor go to a play together; but let us be very strange and well bred; let us be as strange as if we had been married a great while, and as well bred as if we were not married at all.

MIRABELL: Have you any more conditions to offer? Hitherto your demands are pretty reasonable.

MILLAMANT: Trifles! As liberty to pay and receive visits to and from whom I please; to write and receive letters, without interrogatories or wry faces on your part. To wear what I please, and choose conversation with regard only to my own taste; to have no obligation upon me to converse with wits that I don't like, because they are your acquaintance, or to be intimate with fools, because they may be your relations. Come to dinner when I please; dine in my dressing room when I'm out of humour, without giving a reason. To have my closet inviolate; to be sole empress of my tea-table, which you must never presume to approach without first

(Scene continued on p. 24)

(Paraphrase continued from p. 21)

MIRABELL: Then I'll get up inside you as early as I want.

MILLAMANT: Oh! Poor old thing, you do it when you can manage it—and, listen to this, I won't have you calling me names when we're married.

MIRABELL: What do you mean, names?

MILLAMANT: Names like wife, spouse, my dear, joy, jewel, love, sweetheart, and all that sickening jargon with which married people are so cloyingly intimate; I couldn't stand that. Good Mirabell, we mustn't be intimate or lovey-dovey, or kiss in public like Sir Francis and Lady Fadler do. Don't let's go out to Hyde Park in a new coach on our first Sunday as newly-weds in order to make everyone gossip about us, and then never do it again, as if we were proud of each other the first week and ashamed of each other forever after. Don't let's call on people together, or go to the theatre together, but let's be distant and well-bred. Let's be as distant as if we'd been married a long time, and as well-bred as if we weren't married at all.

MIRABELL: Do you want to make any more conditions? So far everything you ask is pretty reasonable.

MILLAMANT: Just little unimportant things! Such as the freedom to call on and to receive visits from anyone I like; to correspond without any questions or face-pulling from you. I want to wear whatever I like and talk about whatever I please; I don't want to have to talk to witty socialites that I don't like, just because you know them, or to spend time with idiots just because they happen to be related to you. I want to have dinner when I choose and dine alone in my boudoir when I'm feeling irritable—without having to explain. I want my private room to *be* private, and I want to be in complete charge of my tea-parties, which you must never dream of joining unless you

(Paraphrase continued on p. 25)

(Scene continued from p. 22)

asking leave. And lastly, wherever I am, you shall always knock at the door before you come in. These articles subscribed, if I continue to endure you a little longer, I may by degrees dwindle into a wife.

MIRABELL: Your bill of fare is something advanced in this latter account. Well, have I liberty to offer conditions, that when you are dwindled into a wife, I may not be beyond measure enlarged into a husband?

MILLAMANT: You have free leave. Propose your utmost; speak and spare not.

MIRABELL: I thank you. *Imprimis* then, I covenant that your acquaintance be general; that you admit no sworn confidante, or intimate of your own sex; no she-friend to screen her affairs under your countenance and tempt you to make trial of a mutual secrecy. No decoy-duck to wheedle you a fop, scrambling to the play in a mask; then bring you home in a pretended fright, when you think you shall be found out and rail at me for missing the play, and disappointing the frolic which you had to pick me up and prove my constancy.

MILLAMANT: Detestable *Imprimis*! I go to the play in a mask!

MIRABELL: Item. I article that you continue to like your own face as long as I shall. And while it passes current with me, that you endeavour not to new coin it. To which end, together with all vizards for the day, I prohibit all masks for the night, made of oiled skins and I know not what hog's bones, hare's gall, pig water, and the marrow of a roasted cat. In short, I forbid all commerce with the gentlewoman in whatd'ye call it Court. Item, I shut my doors against all bawds with baskets and penny-worths of muslin, china, fans, atlases etc. Item, when you shall be breeding—

(Scene continued on p. 26)

(Paraphrase continued from p. 23)

have first asked my permission. Lastly, you must always knock at the door of any room I am in. If you agree to these conditions, and if I continue to be able to put up with you, I may, little by little, shrink into a wife.

MIRABELL: Your menu has grown rather longer with these latest additions. Am I free to ask for some conditions of my own, so that when you have shrunk into a wife I'm not too immeasurably swollen into a husband?

MILLAMANT: Feel free. Do your worst; don't spare me anything.

MIRABELL: Thank you. In the first place, I contract you to have acquaintances rather than intimates. You should not have a best friend to whom you tell everything, no woman friend who can hide her secrets by using you as an alibi, tempting you to do the same. No woman friend drawing public attention away from you as she sets you up with an escort, with whom you attend the theatre in undignified disorder, masked. No woman friend to bring you home when you think you are going to be caught, pretending to be frightened and attacking me for not coming to the play and spoiling your little plan to make me jealous and prove my fidelity.

MILLAMANT: What a hateful contract! As if I would ever go to a play wearing a mask!

MIRABELL: Number one, I formally propose that you admire your face as much as I do, and that you don't try to change it for as long as it continues to please me. So, along with the masks you wear in the day-time, I ban all night-time face-packs consisting of oiled skins and God knows what else—boar's bones, hare's liver, pig's piss, and the bone marrow of a roasted cat. In short, I forbid you to deal with the saleswoman in whatsit Court. Number two, I refuse to admit gypsies with their baskets of wares: cheap muslin, china, fans, silks, etc. Number three, when you are pregnant—

(Paraphrase continued on p. 27)

(Scene continued from p. 24)

MILLAMANT: Ah! —name it not.

MIRABELL: Which may be presumed, with a blessing on our endeavours—

MILLAMANT: Odious endeavours!

MIRABELL: I denounce against all strait-lacing, squeezing for a shape, till you mould my boy's head like a sugar-loaf; and instead of a man-child, make me the father to a crooked billet. Lastly, to the dominion of the tea-table, I submit—but with proviso that you exceed not in your province, but restrain yourself to native and simple tea-table drinks, as tea, chocolate and coffee. As likewise to genuine and authorised tea-table talk, such as mending of fashions, spoiling reputations, railing at absent friends, and so forth; but that on no account you encroach upon the men's prerogative and presume to drink healths, or toast fellows; for prevention of which, I banish all foreign forces, all auxiliaries to the tea-table, as orange brandy, all aniseed, cinnamon, citron and Barbados waters, together with ratafia and the most noble spirit of clary. But for cowslip wine, poppywater and all dormitives, those I allow. These provisos admitted, in other things I may prove a tractable and complying husband.

MILLAMANT: O horrid provisos! Filthy strong waters! I toast fellows, odious men! I hate your odious provisos.

MIRABELL: Then we're agreed. Shall I kiss your hand upon the contract?

(Paraphrase continued from p. 25)

MILLAMANT: Don't even mention it.

MIRABELL: Which is to be expected if our efforts go well—

MILLAMANT: Disgusting efforts!

MIRABELL: I vehemently oppose the lacing of corsets, squeezing your body into shape until you mould my baby boy's head into a cone, and make me the father of a twisted stick instead of a boy. Lastly, I concede your power over the tea-table, with these exceptions. Don't overdo it, restrain yourself to the appropriate tea-table drinks, like tea, chocolate and coffee. Similarly, limit your conversation to talk appropriate to the tea-table, like improving fashions, wrecking reputations, condemning people behind their backs, and so on. On no account trespass into the male sphere and dare to drink healths or propose toasts. In order to prevent this, I ban all inappropriate additions to the tea-table, such as orange brandy, aniseed, cinnamon, citron and flavoured brandy, as well as ratafia and brandy flavoured with clary flowers. But I permit cowslip wine, poppy-water, and all sedative drinks. If you agree to these conditions, I may turn out to be a husband who is pliable and agreeable about other matters.

MILLAMANT: Horrible contradictions! Revolting stimulating drinks! As if I would drink toasts to fellows, to disgusting men! I hate your disgusting exceptions.

MIRABELL: Then we agree. Shall I kiss your hand to seal the deal?

THE WAY OF THE WORLD
Act IV, Scene 1
COMMENTARY

MILLAMANT: **Ay, ay; ha, ha, ha!**
　　　　Like Phoebus sung the no less amorous boy.

Millamant's improbable and unsuitable admirer, Willful, has just asked to take his leave, hence the two eager "ays" from her; and then he's gone—hence the peal of relieved laughter. He was ridiculous and she wanted him to go. Throughout the scene with him she was reciting little bits of poetry, none of which he recognised or understood. This one is a line by Waller, ironically comparing his wooing to that of Phoebus (Apollo) the sun god.

　　[*Enter* MIRABELL.]

MIRABELL: *Like Daphne she as lovely and as coy.* **Do you lock yourself up from me, to make my search more curious? Or is this pretty artifice contrived to signify that here the chase must end and my pursuit be crowned, for you can fly no further?**

Mirabell, her potential other half, is able to supply the other half of the couplet comparing her to a wood-nymph. What sort of effect does that have on her, and how quickly can she hide it?

　　The end of the chase and the crowning of Mirabell's pursuit sound to me like pretty heavy sexual innuendo. "Here we are, we've reached the end of the line, madam. THIS IS IT." That must set up a *frisson*, a tingling sensation down the spine, between them. If we had the erotic scarf in play, this would merit a definite tug from each.

MILLAMANT: **Vanity! No—I'll fly and be followed to the last moment. Though I am upon the very**

> **verge of matrimony, I expect you should solicit me as much as if I were wavering at the grate of a monastery, with one foot over the threshold. I'll be solicited to the very last, nay, and afterwards.**

It's no accident that Millamant should employ a simile involving a monastery! But whose temperature is she trying to lower?

The grate of a monastery or convent was a barred gate to keep out intruders. In nunneries it was too small for the average man to enter.

The punctuation of this speech varies considerably from edition to edition. Here is another published version: "I'll fly and be followed to the last moment, though I am upon the very verge of matrimony; I expect you should solicit me as much as if I were wavering at the grate of a monastery, with one foot over the threshold." Some versions are unactable and provide classic examples of an academic sitting in his study and not considering the problem of communicating to an audience. Erratic punctuation was quite normal in seventeenth- and eighteenth-century play manuscripts. The version printed was often originally taken down by stage management presumably distracted by other duties. So don't take anything as gospel. If it seems hard to make sense of it, take out all the punctuation and start again. (I do not recommend this for later plays: a writer such as George Bernard Shaw was a punctuation fetishist and an actor ignores those precious signals at his peril.)

MIRABELL: What, after the last?

What *is* the last? I don't think it's death. Given Mirabell's state of mind and his capacity for innuendo, I think it means "the ultimate," i.e., even after he's finally got her into bed.

> **MILLAMANT: Oh, I should think I was poor and had nothing to bestow, if I were reduced to an inglorious ease and freed from the agreeable fatigues of solicitation.**

Congreve gives the actress playing Millamant a big present here—the combination of vowels in "the agreeable fatigues of solicitation." It's onomatopoeic, and its suggestiveness should affect Mirabell like a massage. (Both characters' sexual antennae are alert. They miss nothing—their ability to conceal their reactions effectively is part of the erotic game. They *feel* and they control—not always quite in time.)

> MIRABELL: **But do not you know that when favours are conferred upon instant and tedious solicitation that they diminish in their value, and that both the giver loses the grace, and the receiver lessens his pleasure?**

Mirabell picks her up on the topic of flirtation, but is never so crude as to suggest that it is of personal relevance. In any case, he has no critical faculty where Millamant is concerned. It's one of his greatest charms, and an actor playing the part must take his Act I, scene 1 speech as the spine of his relationship with Millamant:. "...I like her with all her faults, nay, like her for her faults. Her follies are so natural, or so artful, that they become her; and those affectations which in another woman would be odious, serve but to make her more agreeable."

There is a word here which has clearly changed its meaning since Congreve's day, for "instant and tedious" seem to a modern ear to be oddly yoked opposites. In fact, "instant" meant "instantly thought of" and therefore "trivial." "Trivial and tedious" are ideas that go readily together, and it would be easy to show through inflection that one word reinforces the other.

> MILLAMANT: **It may be in things of common application, but never sure in love. Oh, I hate a lover that can dare to think he draws a moment's air independent on the bounty of his mistress. There is not so impudent a thing in nature as the saucy look of an assured man, confident of success. The pedantic arrogance of a very husband has not so pragmatical an air. Ah! I'll never marry, unless I am first made sure of my will and pleasure.**

Millamant's exclamations are always clues worth examining. Here her "Oh" provides a launch-pad for a wonderfully capricious attack on the male sex in general; she can't stand men who seem sexually confident, which conceals a particular warning to Mirabell— "Don't ever be too sure of me."

Another word that has changed its meaning since the seventeenth century is "pragmatical," which now means "practical" but here means "conceited." What do you do? You give the merest physical clue to the meaning—no more than that which you would give if you actually used the word "conceited"—and the audience will get it.

The end of Millamant's speech provides a supreme example of repartee.[1] Mirabell capitalises on what she has just said, turning it to his advantage. He takes over her two ideas, "will" and "pleasure," but without repeating the words again; he merely says "the first" and "the other." This means that the actress has to "serve them up" so indelibly that the audience can hang on to the sense and get Mirabell's suggestive joke. "Do you want them both at once or will you have your way now and wait for your sexual pleasure until after we are married?" His laugh is entirely dependent on her delivery. It's not fashionable to discuss these things in rehearsal, but laughs are a matter of cause and effect, and it seems to me we ought to discuss those effects that are mutual territory.

> MIRABELL: **Would you have 'em both before marriage? Or will you he contented with the first now, and stay for the other till after grace?**

This is quick-witted stuff, and no doubt Mirabell is enjoying his own repartee as well as his anticipation of the effect his slightly risqué joke will have on Millamant. But don't forget the erotic potential of the fact that he is basically saying, "Shall I pleasure you now or not?"

> MILLAMANT: **Ah, don't be impertinent! My dear liberty,**

---

[1] For further discussion of repartee, see Chapter 3.

shall I leave thee? My, faithful solitude, my darling contemplation, must I bid you then adieu? Ay-h adieu, my morning thoughts, agreeable wakings, indolent slumbers, all ye douceurs, ye sommeils du matin adieu.—I can't do it, 'tis more than impossible. Positively, Mirabell, I'll lie a-bed in a morning as long as I please.

Another exclamation that's a clue. I think she's thrilled by the idea, but form makes her scold him. I feel the "Ah" is where she dissolves with pleasure herself, and "Don't be impertinent" is the cover she quickly pulls over such a revealing lapse. It's a hilarious slalom from one mood to another. But it needn't necessarily be a swift reaction, that "Ah." A pause before she says it could work very well. A pause is always permissable as long as an angel is beating its wings in it (as long as something crucial is going on in it). Lovers' silences are often extremely meaningful. These two could be quite impassive after his question and before her response, but if our Millamant and Mirabell have created the right kind of force-field of sexual energy then we will be on tenterhooks for her reply. We know by now that the slightest gesture by one is picked up by the other, that none of the remarks miss their destination, and even though there may be very little physical movement in the scene, cause and effect are clearly evident and make a kind of movement of their own.

Now she goes into a most interesting riff. It's my impression that it's a deliberate revenge for the spasm he's just given her. What capital an actress can make with that extraordinary sound "ay-h"! Make sure you don't neglect the "h"—it makes you exhale. I've never seen that exclamation anywhere else. Maggie Smith made a sound like a baby camel being taken from its mother. It implies a sort of sensuous regret for what she is going to have to give up to be a married woman, because there follows an erotic catalogue calculated to drive a man mad. She takes this trivial thing, staying in bed late, and blows it up into something magnificently desirable. The clue is in the language: you cannot say this list of bedroom activities quickly. It's another massage. And then there's a magnificent slalom—"I can't do it." Bang. Short sounds. Abrupt end to massage. She whizzes 'round a corner, leaving him gasping.

> MIRABELL: **Then I'll get up in a morning as early as I please.**

But he hasn't forgotten the rules of repartee—the play is on her "late," for which he substitutes "early." However, after her speech, you can't really blame him for the double meaning on "get up," one of which is explicitly sexual—she's got him all wound up. *Double entendre* (a phrase conveying a double meaning, usually sexual) requires an extraordinary lightness of touch. It gives the actor a special power, like an aside, because it invites the audience to share in a conspiracy.

> MILLAMANT: **Ah! Idle creature, get up when you will— and d'ye hear, I won't be called names after I'm married; positively I won't be called names.**

An exclamation on its own—exploit it to the hilt. Millamant is confronting the unadorned idea of making love to him.

The next line puzzled me for a long time, because it's not strictly logical. I know Millamant is flustered, but cogent repartee is such a reflex to these two, one would imagine that self-betraying "Ah!" would be all she would need before climbing back into the saddle. What perplexed me was that he says he'll get up *early* and she calls him *idle*. Idle people get up late, don't they? I put it down to her general confusion and I never looked it up in the *OED*. Then one day I was giving a master class in Oxford, and a professor of English literature told me that "idle" could also mean "impotent" in the seventeenth century. So it emerges that Millamant, far from being thrown, is making a brilliant and conversation-stopping comeback. She's saying, "You poor old thing, you just get it up whenever you can manage it..." Incidentally, she's also showing herself to be a true woman of the Restoration:

they were conversationally liberated. She takes a sexy remark on the chin and gives back as good as she gets. Her moods are wonderfully volatile—one moment she's a puddle of feeling and the next she's tossing off a coarse remark with the best of them.

Then comes a lightning change of tack, possibly because that put-down has been so successful that it enables her to move on; puts her in charge of the agenda. She is empowered to change the subject; the abruptness with which she does it shows she has been feeling the strain.

MIRABELL: **Names!**

It's so abrupt that even Mirabell is taken aback.

MILLAMANT: **Ay, as wife, spouse, my dear, joy, jewel, love, sweetheart and the rest of that nauseous cant in which men and their wives are so fulsomely familiar; I shall never bear that. Good Mirabell, don't let us be familiar or fond, nor kiss before folks, like my Lady Fadler and Sir Francis; nor go to Hyde Park together the first Sunday in a new chariot, to provoke eyes and whispers, and then never to be seen there together again, as if we were proud of one another the first week, and ashamed of one another for ever after. Let us never visit together, nor go to a play together; but let us be very strange and well bred; let us be as strange as if we had been married a great while, and as well bred as if we were not married at all.**

One has to seek opportunities to distinguish one's attitude to each item in the catalogue, without *over*-colouring so that it ceases to be a list, becoming instead a sort of pace-destroying contemplation of each ingredient. Since Millamant says these names make her feel sick, it's always struck me that one of the list might actually make her throat constrict. Or that she can hardly bring herself to articulate one of them. Or that having uttered one, she can't forbear a little moan of horror. But you can't take the time to comment on all of them!

I don't think Millamant is trying anything on here. This is a very sincere and honest approach to Mirabell about something which is important to her. She is telling him for the first time what she really wants—her "will" as opposed to her "pleasure." She's a refined spirit and she doesn't want them to make a vulgar display of anything as precious as their love. The fact that she calls Mirabell "Good Mirabell" implies to me that she feels that if he is as good as she believes him to be then he will agree with her.

"Faddling" means "fondling" and gives an onomatopoeic picture even now of a couple patting and paddling at each other. But although the image of the Fadlers is comedic one, the subject is serious to Millamant. Is it as important to Mirabell? Experiment with the degree of his agreement and see how it affects the speech. Experiment with the Fadlers themselves. Actors need to establish their attitudes to characters in the script who never appear on stage. Does Mirabell know these people? Does he know how they behave in public already? Or does he gradually put a name to a face, have to be persuaded that they are distasteful? These decisions will profoundly affect how Millamant sets about persuading him of her argument.

"Strange" here means distant, as in estranged, rather than peculiar.

MIRABELL: **Have you any more conditions to offer? Hitherto your demands are pretty reasonable.**

What she wants is what he wants. But did he make her wait for his verdict? Or is he a little suspicious that it all seems a bit too straightforward to be true?

MILLAMANT: **Trifles! –As liberty to pay and receive visits to and from whom I please; to write and receive letters, without interrogatories or wry faces on your part. To wear what I please, and choose conversation with regard only to my own taste; to have no obligation upon me to converse with wits that I don't like, because they are your acquaintance, or to be intimate with fools, because they may be your**

relations. Come to dinner when I please; dine in my dressing room when I'm out of humour, without giving a reason. To have my closet inviolate; to be sole empress of my tea-table, which you must never presume to approach without first asking leave. And lastly, wherever I am, you shall always knock at the door before you come in. These articles subscribed, if I continue to endure you a little longer, I may by degrees dwindle into a wife.

If I were in the audience, Millamant's timing on this first word would tell me everything I wanted to know. If she came in very quickly with that cue, then I would know that she had worked out all her conditions beforehand, and that they were not trifles at all, at least not to her. Or if she hesitated, shrugging prettily, before choosing exactly the right word to show how mightily unimportant these conditions are, then "Trifles!" would be a *dangerously* careless exclamation.

Another list. As an exercise, you might treat the speech as if she had a prepared list which she whips out of her pocket. Then you will see that there are certain phrases that seem to be spontaneous, that are unlikely to be prepared because they arise from something that Mirabell is doing. For example, "without wry faces or interrogatories on your part" seems to be quashing a current interruption. What happens *in the moment* is always more interesting on stage, so even if Millamant has merely prepared her conditions in her head and there is no actual list on paper, what will bring the "trifles" to life is the interaction between her and Mirabell. Improvise interruptions from Mirabell while Millamant sticks to the text and see how it colors her speech. You will make all kinds of discoveries if you play around with the possibilities. Imagine how it helps Millamant's timing and spontaneity if her Mirabell, in response to her request to dine in her dressing-room when she is out of humour, asks indignantly, "Why?" and she can crack back, "*without* giving a reason." Or Millamant may be amazed at one point to get by with no opposition to a condition she thought would provoke an uproar; at another point Mirabell may be trigger happy about a condition that she thought was totally reasonable. You will not use all these options when you return to the text, but the temporary duologue you created will have permeated your consciousness in such a way that you will be highly attuned to each other's minute reactions for ever after. This speech, like all speeches, is not just the property of its speaker.

It's a charming, capricious idea to preserve intimacy by distance. She wants her mystery. So, wherever I am, you must knock...

"These articles subscribed" is the formal language of contracts.

The sound of the word "endure" contradicts its meaning: it's a word to wallow in and enjoy. So the choice of word, while not precisely onamatopoeic, is the onomatopoeia of her psyche, because she is going to adore enduring Mirabell. Then she checks herself three times in her approach to that nauseating word "wife": "I may/by degrees/dwindle/into a wife." Congreve does all the work here. "Endure" betrays itself by the sound, then a sidle up to that great verb "dwindle"—the result is a glorious built-in irony.

Dame Edith Evans was a famous Millamant. When she was very old, a friend went to see her recital of extracts from great parts she had played. Just before the curtain went up, a well-known actress in the audience tapped my friend on the shoulder. "I've come for *dwindle*," she said. "What have you come for?"

MIRABELL: **Your bill of fare is something advanced in this latter account. Well, have I liberty to offer conditions, that when you are dwindled into a wife, I may not be beyond measure enlarged into a husband?**

Very sexy stuff, so overt [enlarged = with an erection] that it's probably best done dead pan. The laugh comes with the effect it has on Millamant, which takes place in the pause before she has collected herself. I call a pause like this a "ping," i.e., a pause with a sting in it.

MILLAMANT: **You have free leave. Propose your utmost; speak and spare not.**

Brisk. Suspiciously brisk. She has to be brisk, she has to be prim, because she has to turn the talk away from the bawdiness that makes her weak at the knees. It's a major change of tone. And why does she say more or less the same thing three times? Is Mirabell crowding her, deliberately misinterpreting "you have free leave" as a physical invitation?

> **MIRABELL: I thank you.** *Imprimis* **then, I covenant that your acquaintance be general; that you admit no sworn confidante, or intimate of your own sex; no she-friend to screen her affairs under your countenance and tempt you to make trial of a mutual secrecy. No decoy-duck to wheedle you a fop, scrambling to the play in a mask; then bring you home in a pretended fright, when you think you shall be found out and rail at me for missing the play, and disappointing the frolic which you had to pick me up and prove my constancy.**

He picks up—or parodies?—her formal tone. He abandons the sexual trajectory and moves into legal language with the term "imprimis" (pronounced "impreemis"). This is an extremely difficult speech and a real hurdle for the actor playing Mirabell. Almost the only way it works is fast, as it is a sort of fantasy scenario which tells a story in one long sentence. But of course its elements have to be fully comprehended by the actor before he can get up to speed, or an audience will be utterly bemused. So paraphrase, and make sure you grasp all the social ramifications. (Married women were frequently adulterous; Mirabell is defying the convention by saying he won't put up with it. A fop was not necessarily an effeminate man, but an overdressed danger to the female sex. Prostitutes wore masks, so any woman who wore one in a public place was proclaiming her intentions.) Then see the story like a movie running in your head as you say Congreve's words. It's a story about what he doesn't want in his marriage; a story of two women getting deeper and deeper into the mire of deception. Do this speech until you can effortlessly communicate its meaning. It takes good breath control, because driving through the story, keeping its elements connected is what makes it work, but if your brain disconnects from the narrative for an instant the whole thing disintegrates into meaninglessness.

"Wheedle" and "scrambling" are more presents from Congreve—wonderful verbs to propel the story forward—and one tip is to keep the confidante, the intimate, the she-friend, the decoy-duck, and the person who brings her home as the same woman in your mental picture. This scenario is an entirely accurate description of married life of the time; many women behaved indiscreetly and then turned situations to their own advantage in the face of discovery. "I was only pretending to be unfaithful as a test of your interest in me."

While it's far from the only possible pattern of emphasis, I have noticed that if Mirabell indignantly hits "rail at *me*" the narrative is clearer.

MILLAMANT: Detestable *Imprimis*! I go to the play in a mask!

Millamant combats this in a wonderfully oblique way. She picks on a detail—"You can't think that I'd be so vulgar as to go to a play in a mask. So obviously the story isn't about me." She doesn't say that his condition is unreasonable and she doesn't disagree with it. She permits it while pointing out that it has nothing to do with her.

MIRABELL: Item. I article that you continue to like your own face as long as I shall. And while it passes current with me, that you endeavour not to new coin it. To which end, together with all vizards for the day, I prohibit all masks for the night, made of oiled skins and I know not what hog's bones, hare's gall, pig water, and the marrow of a roasted cat. In short, I forbid all commerce with the gentlewoman in whatd'ye call it Court. Item, I shut my doors against all bawds with baskets and penny-worths of muslin, china, fans, atlases etc. Item, when you shall be breeding—

"Item" is the same sort of legalese as "imprimis" and cloaks Mirabell's seriousness about apparently trivial matters, just as "trifles" cloaked Millamant's. Try the device of her reacting vocally to his list of requirements, because he uses those later "item"s as a guillotine for potential interruptions.

There is a particular problem with the word "atlases" which meant "small bolts of silk" in Congreve's day. Since it has a modern meaning which makes sense in context, I don't see the point in struggling for the period meaning. One gets the idea that old hags were selling unnecessary stuff door to door.

> MILLAMANT: Ah! —name it not.

Too much for Millamant's sensibility; she hasn't even got married yet.

> MIRABELL: Which may be presumed, with a blessing on
> our endeavours—

He is *relentless* in his attempts to make her blush. One can imagine him grinning with delight at the success of the previous sally.

> MILLAMANT: Odious endeavours!

She cuts him off before he can go any further, but I think Congreve is giving us the psychological truth through onomatopoeia again. She is saying one thing and meaning another.

> MIRABELL: I denounce against all strait-lacing, squeezing for a shape, till you mould my boy's head like a sugar-loaf; and instead of a man-child, make me the father to a crooked billet. Lastly, to the dominion of the tea-table, I submit—but with proviso that you exceed not in your province, but restrain yourself to native and simple tea-table drinks, as tea, chocolate and coffee. As likewise to genuine and authorised tea-table talk, such as mending of fashions, spoiling reputations, railing at absent friends, and so forth; but that on no account you encroach upon the men's prerogative and presume

to drink healths, or toast fellows; for prevention of which, I banish all foreign forces, all auxiliaries to the tea-table, as orange brandy, all aniseed, cinnamon, citron and Barbados waters, together with ratafia and the most noble spirit of clary. But for cowslip wine, poppywater and all dormitives, those I allow. These provisos admitted, in other things I may prove a tractable and complying husband.

Mirabell gives us a bit more social history here—babies were born deformed because of their mother's corsets—and as usual, his ideas are radical. (No masks, no face-packs, no confidantes, no saleswomen coming to the house, no corsets.) His tea-table conditions, at first glance rather mystifying, boil down to this: he doesn't want her to get excitable or masculine. Her blood courses through her veins quite fast enough and she is quite liberated enough in her conversation as it is. The male tradition of drinking toasts was to swill bumper upon bumper of wine, usually in celebration of some actual or hoped-for sexual conquest. Mirabell doesn't want her mixed up in anything licentious.

> MILLAMANT: **O horrid provisos! Filthy strong waters! I toast fellows, odious men! I hate your odious provisos.**

Millamant uses the same technique as before about the mask, implying that she would never be caught dead drinking strong drink or toasting anyone. She doesn't disagree.

> MIRABELL: **Then we're agreed. Shall I kiss your hand upon the contract?**

Mirabell understands her code perfectly.

ENERGY

Energy can be a confusing word in the context of acting. It's not necessarily physical at all. You can be completely immobile and still give off sparks of energy. What grabs an audience's attention is immediacy. This is achieved by concentration, and, as in almost any other field, concentration proves to be its own reward—the concentration of an actor lures the concentration of an audience. In high comedy, or any other kind of play for that matter, there is only one moment and that moment is now. You must engage with that moment, thinking down the middle of the thought as you are saying it. Sometimes you will be saying one thing and thinking another, since high comedy is full of irony, but in every case you cannot permit yourself any anticipation or any retrospection. If you give your full attention to this connection of brain and tongue, then you make the spark. You'll notice this was part of my recipe for naturalism as well, but energy and naturalism are inseparable in high comedy, because what we are trying to achieve is a heightened realism.

A special demand is made on energy by high comedy, because you have to be in an intensified state to play it. It's as if you have to work at a higher temperature than normal. In rehearsal, if you need to heave your performance up a notch in energy terms (and, incidentally, to respond to that bewildering directorial request "give me *more*"), then sing it. A rehearsal spent turning the text into grand opera can leave a vestige of bravura in its wake that is really useful to modern actors struggling for *brio*. Or briefly adopting an exotic foreign accent can give one the courage to experience the power of heightened being.

Sustaining this bubble of special energy can be particularly hard on a first night or in performance. Anyone who has ever been in a musical will know how grateful one feels for the overture, which not only whips up one's pulse with anticipation, but provides a microcosm of the whole evening which is to follow; a little taste of all its ingredients. Plays require us to create our own overture to get us into a state of readiness to step on that stage. There are many schools of thought on how to achieve this state. To read Lee Strasberg on how Mrs. Siddons (1755–1831) and Stanislavsky dealt with it is to straddle several centuries of the problem:

> Mrs. Siddons, who was probably the greatest Lady Macbeth of all time, has told how, when she played certain parts, she would stand backstage and watch the play before she made her entrance; otherwise she could not act the scene. She didn't know about getting into the scene the way that we pretend to know. She didn't know about the psychology of imagination. She didn't know about concentration as a definable element of consciousness. She didn't know any of the things that Stanislavsky and others have brought to our attention. She knew only the actor's problem of appealing to his imagination. She, one of the greatest actresses of all time, had the same difficulty of whipping herself into a scene, of getting herself in the mood, of starting herself in the play that we do.

Notice how Lee Strasberg resorts to three attempts to describe exactly *what* Mrs. Siddons is doing. I prefer to sidle up to it by looking first at the result: definition and attack. What these two ingredients require to back them up is that hideously elusive commodity, confidence. Confidence primarily in whom and what you are playing and the manner in which you are playing (rehearsal will have established these, but the results may be ebbing from you in the wings), and secondarily in the fact that those things will be intrinsically believable to an audience. I haven't read any writers on acting who are frank about this disabling doubt that can assail the actor about perfectly sound choices. You cannot afford to be distracted from your primary task by a rustle or a cough; you must be secure in the knowledge that you are not only real but *fascinating*. I've always found it necessary to employ a little trickery to achieve this, and I suspect that most actors lack the self-confidence that is required here. In the dressing room, try using some of your lines to express the following:

✧ I think I'm terrific, and I expect you'll come to the same conclusion pretty soon.

✧ I see right through you.

✧ I am explaining the obvious. Are you intelligent enough to grasp that?

✧ I am expressing myself quite brilliantly.

The effect of this exercise is to kill off any tentativeness. You can summon up the memory of this authority as you stand in the wings. Technically, it means that you attack the front end of a sentence as if you mean business, instead of creepng up apologetically. Psychologically it puts you in control of your material. If you know what you're doing, do it. It won't be over the top, it will simply have the requisite energy. Under-acting produces a lazy portrait of reality. If you're in possession of the thought, then you are in charge of what you say, so why shouldn't your voice reflect that confidence? John Barrymore's definition of acting is going to hold good for high comedy for a few centuries more—"Acting is the art of saying a thing on the stage as if you believed every word you utter to be as true as the eternal verities of life; it is the art of doing a thing on the stage as if the logic of the thing demanded that precise act and no other; and of doing and saying the thing as spontaneously as if you were confronted with the situation in which you were acting for the first time."

"The Illusion of the First Time" is a phrase created by William Gillette in 1915 and is still the most basic demand made of the actor. My old enemy Anticipation quite destroys it. Energy and concentration on the moment sustain it. Without the illusion that everything happening in front of an audience is new-minted, engaging their imaginations with its spontaneity, then they might as well be at some weary old burlesque show. It's really hard work to invent spontaneity in the first place, much less sustain it. You must cultivate the oblique approach, the unusual reaction, find ways of simulating life with all its contradictions and inconsequentialties.

Being specific takes energy. You must have a clear image in

your head of everything that you refer to in the text. If you have, the audience will. It's a simple equation, but hard to execute without faltering or distraction. I was in *The Women* by Clare Booth Luce at the Old Vic Theatre in London. It has a cast of about thirty, all women. The play consists of their relationships to men— they dissect them, betray them, divorce them, outwit them—but not a single man ever appears on the stage. So the actresses brought in photographs that represented their men and showed them to everyone playing a woman who would know them. My character, Sylvia, was complacent about her marriage, not knowing that her husband was unfaithful. I chose a picture of Danny de Vito as my husband. I am very tall, so whenever anybody spoke of us as a couple or visualised us together, a sort of smirk crept over her face because of the vision she had of this incongruous physical coupling. And it made it absolutely clear that everyone was discussing the same person. You might think that's a tiny detail, but it makes an enormous difference to the texture of the piece.

Collaborative personalisation will prove useful for this extract from one of the gossip scenes in *A School for Scandal* by Richard Brinsley Sheridan. Characters are talked about who never appear in the play. Since the gossips pounce on each of their victims with avidity, we must find a way to infuse modern actors with the same relish.

There are three of these scenes distributed throughout the play and they are quite self-contained. They advance the action very little: only Lady Teazle and Lady Sneerwell are involved in the main plot. But the gossips create the moral world of the play; the malignant backdrop against which the rest is played out. Through them we see clearly what kind of behaviour gets rewarded in this society, and what gets you ostracised. This is a pack. They are disparate people, but they have the pack's capacity to tear a victim apart.

From elsewhere in the play, we learn information that is relevant here. Sir Benjamin Backbite and his uncle Mr. Crabtree have a relationship that turns sour under a certain provocation. When

Sir Benjamin gets a bit too witty and a bit too adept at producing the juiciest tit-bits of gossip, Crabtree resents it. But neither takes anything personally for very long—they're too caught up in the pursuit of scandal.

Lady Sneerwell is the most dangerous one in the group and the most embittered. She is the top dog socially. She is jealous of Lady Teazle.

Mrs. Candour is a hypocrite—she very nearly succeeds in bringing off the illusion of being a woman of propriety who really dislikes gossip. But underneath she is salivating for the next titillating detail.

Lady Teazle is the new girl in the group, working hard to show she can play their game as well as they can. She's keen to acquire the affectations of a sophisticate.

THE SCHOOL FOR SCANDAL

BY RICHARD BRINSLEY SHERIDAN

Act II, Scene 2

MRS. CANDOUR: Now I'll die, but you are so scandalous I'll forswear your society.

LADY TEAZLE: What's the matter, Mrs. Candour?

MRS. CANDOUR: They'll not allow our friend Miss Vermilion to be handsome.

LADY SNEERWELL: Oh, surely she is a pretty woman.

CRABTREE: I am very glad you think so, ma'am.

MRS. CANDOUR: She has a charming fresh colour.

LADY TEAZLE: Yes, when it is fresh put on.

MRS. CANDOUR: Oh, fie. I'll swear her colour is natural: I have seen it come and go.

LADY TEAZLE: I daresay you have, ma'am: it goes off at night and comes again in the morning.

SIR BENJAMIN: True, ma'am, it not only comes and goes, but, what's more, egad, her maid can fetch and carry it.

MRS. CANDOUR: Ha, ha, ha! How I hate to hear you talk so! But surely now, her sister is–or was–very handsome.

CRABTREE: Who, Mrs. Evergreen? Oh, lord, she's six and fifty if she's an hour.

MRS. CANDOUR: Now positively you wrong her. Fifty-two or fifty-three is the utmost and I don't think she looks more.

SIR BENJAMIN: Ah, there is no judging by her looks unless one could see her face.

LADY SNEERWELL: Well, well, if Mrs. Evergreen does take some pains to repair the ravages of time, you must allow she effects it with great ingenuity; and surely that's better than the careless manner in which the widow Ochre caulks her wrinkles.

SIR BENJAMIN: Nay, now, Lady Sneerwell, you are severe upon the widow. Come, come, 'tis not that she paints so ill but when she has finished her face, she joins it on so badly to her neck that she looks like a mended statue, in which the connoisseur sees at once that the head's modern, though the trunk's antique.

CRABTREE: Ha, ha, ha! Well said, nephew!

MRS. CANDOUR: Ha, ha, ha! Well, you make me laugh, but I vow I hate you for it. What do you think of Miss Simper?

SIR BENJAMIN: Why, she has very pretty teeth.

LADY TEAZLE: Yes, and on that account, when she is neither speaking nor laughing (which very seldom happens), she never absolutely shuts her mouth, but leaves it always on a jar, as it were, thus. [*Shows her teeth.*]

MRS. CANDOUR: How can you be so ill-natured?

LADY TEAZLE: Nay, I allow even that's better than the pains Mrs. Prim takes to conceal her losses in front. She draws her mouth till it positively resembles the aperture of a poor's-box and all her words appear to slide out edgewise, as it were thus, How do you do, madam? Yes, madam.

LADY SNEERWELL: Very well, Lady Teazle; I see you can be a little severe.

THE SCHOOL FOR SCANDAL

Act II, Scene 2

COMMENTARY

MRS. CANDOUR: **Now I'll die, but you are so scandalous I'll forswear your society!**

LADY TEAZLE: **What's the matter, Mrs. Candour?**

MRS. CANDOUR: **They'll not allow our friend Miss Vermilion to be handsome.**

Mrs. Candour starts the scene with a fairly plausible display of disapproval, but she is easily led into repeating what earned her apparent disapproval in the first place. She is, in a manner of speaking, throwing gossip-fodder to the big fat trout in the gossip pool. Each topic has to be launched. Then the trout all surge to the surface in pursuit of the tit-bit. Everything that follows is a kind of repartee, in the sense that each person caps or capitalises on what has gone before.

LADY SNEERWELL: **Oh, surely she is a pretty woman.**

Lady Sneerwell's comment is not innocent—the "surely" demands an answer and therefore confirms that Miss Vermilion is a promising subject for discussion.

CRABTREE: **I am very glad you think so, ma'am.**

Crabtree is on to her mock-admiration in a flash and raises the stakes with *his* mock admiration of her view. There is an unspoken "because nobody else does" at the end of his line.

MRS. CANDOUR: **She has a charming fresh colour.**

Mrs. Candour refuels the discussion with another apparently innocent defence of Miss Vermilion, but of course what she is actually doing is providing fodder for the gossips.

LADY TEAZLE: **Yes, when it is fresh put on.**

She gets a pert repartee from the eager Lady Teazle.

MRS. CANDOUR: **Oh, fie. I'll swear her colour is natural:**
I have seen it come and go.

"Oh fie"—is that pain or pleasure? It's the same as "Now I'll die" at the start. All her exclamations are pleasure masquerading as disapproval. Mrs. Candour is a wonderful feed for Lady Teazle. She does it on purpose, but it must be done with the utmost innocence.

LADY TEAZLE: **I daresay you have, ma'am: it goes off at**
night and comes again in the morning.

SIR BENJAMIN: **True, ma'am, it not only comes and**

> **goes, but, what's more, egad, her maid can fetch and carry it.**

Sir Benjamin doesn't add anything new, he merely reinforces Lady Teazle's remark, but he impresses himself. He punctuates his thought with a little exclamation at his own cleverness, "What's more, egad."

> MRS. CANDOUR: **Ha, ha, ha! How I hate to hear you talk so! But surely now, her sister is—or was—very handsome.**

Mrs. Candour has to slam the lid on her spontaneous laughter with a lightening return to hypocrisy. Then she launches a new topic by introducing Mrs. Evergreen into the conversation. "Is, *or was*, very handsome"—she's baiting them with that little bit of uncertainty and disloyalty.

> CRABTREE: **Who, Mrs Evergreen? Oh lord, she's six and fifty if she's an hour.**

> MRS. CANDOUR: **Now positively you wrong her. Fifty-two or fifty-three is the utmost and I don't think she looks more.**

In her next line she uses another variation of the same tactic. If she'd stopped at "at the utmost," the topic would have been closed. But if she emphasises "I" or "think" in the next statement, then she opens up the whole debate again. It's not a big piece of gossip-fodder, but she is definitely trailing a crumb across the surface of the gossip pool.

> SIR BENJAMIN: **Ah, there is no judging by her looks unless one could see her face.**

And that fat trout Sir Benjamin shoots right up to grab it. Perhaps this is the moment to point out that they are all keen to score with *bons mots*. So it's not just a question of analysing one's spoken contribution, but of working out why one *doesn't* speak. Pipped at the post? Bored with that subject? Don't know the victim? Slowed down by your jealousy that someone else is being wittier than you? Laughing too much to put your oar in?

> LADY SNEERWELL: **Well, well, if Mrs. Evergreen does take some pains to repair the ravages of time, you must allow she effects it with great ingenuity; and surely that's better than the careless manner in which the widow Ochre caulks her wrinkles.**

Lady Sneerwell wraps up one topic and launches the next. She does the first with an appearance of generosity which may well disappoint her fellow gossips, but she slaloms[3] seamlessly into slander. She was only setting up her own punch line (Ochre is a yellow-brown paint).

> SIR BENJAMIN: **Nay, now, Lady Sneerwell, you are severe upon the widow. Come, come, 'tis not that she paints so ill but when she has finished her face, she joins it on so badly to her neck that she looks like a mended statue, in which the connoisseur sees at once that the head's modern, though the trunk's antique.**

Sir Benjamin uses the same technique as he pretends to chide her for her cruelty, and then slaloms into a massacre of the Widow Ochre's make-up skills that is far crueller. Or maybe Lady Sneerwell and Sir Benjamin are mimicking Mrs. Casndour's sweet charity to amuse the company before swinging into their usual viciousness?

> CRABTREE: **Ha, ha, ha! Well said, nephew!**

Crabtree's compliment to his nephew could be interpreted several ways and will depend on what sort of relationship they have created between them. He could laugh through his teeth, resenting Benjamin's social success, feeling jealous of his vivid demolition job on the widow. He could be amazed that Benjamin could invent such a joke. (Establishing unusual behaviour through the surprise

---

[3] A sudden mood change. This is discussed in depth in Chapter 5.

of others who know the person well is a useful aid to creating a character). He could be genuinely and generously amused.

> MRS. CANDOUR: **Ha, ha, ha! Well, you make me laugh, but I vow I hate you for it. What do you think of Miss Simper?**

Mrs. Candour does another slalom, from a laugh to a protestation of innocence, which is instantly undermined by her launching the topic of Miss Simper.

> SIR BENJAMIN: **Why, she has very pretty teeth.**

Sir Benjamin is on a roll of self-confidence. I should be interested to know what Crabtree thinks of it. Of course, teeth are not the part of the anatomy that send people into ecstasies of admiration, so it's pretty damning that they are Miss Simper's only good point.

> LADY TEAZLE: **Yes, and on that account, when she is neither speaking nor laughing (which very seldom happens), she never absolutely shuts her mouth, but leaves it always on a jar, as it were, thus. [*Shows her teeth.*]**

Lady Teazle seizes her opportunity to shine, probably pipping half the group to the post, and gives a lively demonstration into the bargain.

> MRS. CANDOUR: **How can you be so ill-natured?**

This elicits repressed delight from Mrs. Candour, taking its usual form of jolly reproof.

> LADY TEAZLE: **Nay, I allow even that's better than the pains Mrs. Prim takes to conceal her losses in front. She draws her mouth till it positively resembles the aperture of a poor's-box and all her words appear to slide out edgewise, as it were thus, How do you do, madam? Yes, madam.**

Flushed with her success, Lady Teazle tops her previous performance with a more vigorous demonstration.

> **LADY SNEERWELL: Very well, Lady Teazle; I see you can be a little severe.**

Why does Lady Sneerwell call Lady Teazle "severe"? She's no more severe than anyone else in the group. Is Lady Sneerwell praising her—the novice who is coming along so promisingly in the severity stakes? Is it a put-down because Lady Sneerwell doesn't like Lady Teazle to dominate the group? Is it a manifestation of sexual jealousy?

There is nothing very difficult about Sheridan's language. The difficulty with the scene is that it's not at all physical—in fact, it's probably very static. It's about brains latching on to information. So when a new butt for the gossips' tongues appears in the text, it must be a *palpable* stimulus for all of them; even if their tactic is to affect indifference (Lady Sneerwell) or disapproval (Mrs. Candour).

In the gossip scenes from *The School for Scandal*, characters who never appear in the play are gleefully skewered, but without real energy and enthusiasm the effect can seem strained. As gossip appears to be a perennial human failing, we should exploit it here. Precede the scene with a little improvised gossip of your own, using contemporary figures familiar to all. It can be true or false, about well-known people, or the company, or the director. It should make you slightly aghast at your own indiscretion and daring. The nearer to home it is, the more dangerous and the more useful to the scene. After all, ruthlessness and lies and laughs are what a gossip is addicted to. If you improvise for five minutes or so, the person playing Mrs. Candour will undoubtedly hear something sufficiently amazing to permit her to plunge in with "Now I'll die, but you are so scandalous I'll forswear your society"—and for the scene to begin in a properly excited and anticipatory mood.

If this mood somehow dribbles away, doesn't sustain itself through the text, there is another trick that seems to revitalise everyone's delight in those off-stage characters such as Mrs. Evergreen and the Widow Ochre. The speaker must replace, *without conferring*, the names of the gossip victims with an appropriate modern name familiar to all, for example:

MRS. CANDOUR: . . . But, surely now, her sister is—or was—very handsome?

CRABTREE: Who—Joan Collins? Oh, lord, she's six and fifty if she's an hour.

MRS. CANDOUR: Now positively you wrong her. Fifty two or fifty three is the utmost—and I don't think she looks more.

SIR BENJAMIN: Ah, there is no judging by her looks unless one could see her face.

LADY SNEERWELL: Well, well, if Joan Collins does take some pains to repair the ravages of time, you must allow she affects it with great ingenuity; and surely that's better than the careless manner in which Zsa Zsa Gabor caulks her wrinkles.

SIR BENJAMIN: Nay, now Lady Sneerwell, you are severe upon Zsa Zsa. Come, come, 'tis not that she paints so ill—but when she has finished her face, she joins it on so badly to her neck that she looks like a mended statue, in which the connoisseur sees at once that the head's modern, though the trunk's antique.

Another kind of substitution may be useful in this scene. The question of whether someone uses rouge, or whether her make-up is badly applied, doesn't have much edge for a modern actor. The closest parallel nowadays is probably the question of whether someone has had plastic surgery or not. Play the scene with that substitution and you will observe a whole new range of possibilities: does your character disapprove of cosmetic surgery? has your character undergone it? concealed the fact? etc., etc. Matters of appearance are of great moment in the school for scandal and you must enable yourself to feel their importance.

How do these gossips look? Have they got any of the flaws they are condemning? Do they know it? There is endless mileage here. Lady Sneerwell may dislike references to age; Mrs. Candour may show her teeth in ready smiles until Miss Simper is condemned, and so forth.

I think it is always useful (especially in a scene ostensibly dominated by conversation) to consider what other senses might be engaged. I'd like to know whether my character is too hot or too cold, or whether that changes because of emotion. I'd like to know who smells. The person who does won't know. But if you think Backbite does, then when he passes you his after-draught may cause you to react. It's too easy to shut down the senses in a scene where the talk is lively.

If the director has you eating or drinking or embroidering or any other drawing-room activity that fits his gossip scene, then it's like being given an extra voice. The action can tell the truth: Lady Sneerwell stabbing the embroidery frame while her tone remains creamily polite; Crabtree hiding his lack of enthusiasm for Sir Benjamin's jokes by drinking his tea while the others laugh.

Finding out where the focus should be is always essential, but never more so than in a scene which is filled with characters who would like to steal the focus. Working towards that reality as a character, you may pull the audience's eye towards yourself more than is good for the scene. The director may dismiss all your wonderful creativity as upstaging the real action. Then ask the director where exactly he wants the focus at each moment that is not obvious to you. Sometimes I do an exercise in rehearsal that clarifies this: the actors throw an orange to each other whenever the focus changes. Whoever has the orange has the focus, because we permit each other to have it. Any fool can draw attention away from another actor. The trick is to persist with the energy of your internal life *without* drawing attention to it. This is particularly apposite when you have to deal with an aside (a remark to the audience which the other characters don't hear) by another actor. Life must continue in the scene when one actor steps outside it to deliver his aside. The focus is indisputably on him, but the other characters don't go dead. Their life simply goes on at a lower temperature; it recedes fom the audience's consciousness, allowing the person delivering the aside to dominate. It's those things like smells and body temperature which form your character's sense-existence that prevent one from turning to cardboard at such moments, that enable one to be generously reticent. You know that you're *there* without feeling compelled to overstate the case. You are there because of mental energy.

3

WIT:
Repartee and
Irony

REPARTEE

What does wit demand of the actor? Nobody is asking you to do something mysterious and amorphous like "be funny." Comics can be funny independent of their material. No one can be witty unless the words are witty. So if you say witty words, will you be witty? No, because wit isn't muscular enough to stand up on its own unless your thinking supports it. Understand the thoughts behind the witty words, say them, and you'll be witty? You will have made a start. But we have to draw the audience into the experience of wit, not just the meaning. "*The Way of the World* is not only too witty for real life; it is very probably too witty for the stage. Hearing it spoken, we have to pant to keep up with it." Louis Koningsberg's opinion, expressed in his preface to a collection of comedies, is absurdly negative. *Nothing* is too witty for the stage. If the audience has to pant after us, we are doing it wrong. But if we understand the game and communicate not only the meaning but our relish for the form, the audience will keep up with us, and the experience will make *the audience* witty.

Repartee is a form of wit that is still alive and well, and which particularly suits the cut and thrust of high comedy. A very clear example of it occurs in Shakespeare's *Much Ado About Nothing* in the first scene between Beatrice and Benedick. They are old adversaries who either don't admit or don't realise their attraction for one another, and here they are showing off their mental paces in front of Leonato, the governor of Messina, and his guests and household. In other words, it's a public contest of wit which each wants to win. It's also an effective way of capturing the other's full attention, because repartee is a form of wit that builds on what the other person has just said. So if you're going to win you have to listen like a hawk.

MUCH ADO ABOUT NOTHING

WILLIAM SHAKESPEARE

Act I, Scene 1

BEATRICE: I wonder that you will still be talking, Signior Benedick; nobody marks you.

BENEDICK: What, my dear Lady Disdain! Are you yet living?

BEATRICE: Is it possible Disdain should die, while she hath such meet food to feed it as Signior Benedick? Courtesy itself must convert to Disdain if you come in her presence.

BENEDICK: Then is courtesy a turncoat.* But it is certain I am loved of all ladies, only you excepted; and I would I could find in my heart that I had not a hard heart; for truly I love none.

BEATRICE: A dear happiness to women! They would else have been troubled with a pernicious suitor. I thank God and my

---

* A turncoat is a soldier who turned his uniform inside out so that he could defect to the other side.

(Scene continued on p. 62)

The first hurdle, as always, is the meaning, so paraphrase the speeches into modern English when there is any obscurity. Don't gloss over anything unfamiliar or archaic: worry away at it with a dictionary and footnotes until you are quite sure you understand every word. Here is a literal paraphrase of the scene: your own version may differ in detail, but must not compress or skate over any of the ideas, even if the result is rather inelegant.

✧ ✧ ✧

MUCH ADO ABOUT NOTHING
Act I, Scene 1
PARAPHRASE

BEATRICE: I'm surprised you're still talking, Signior Benedick—nobody's paying you any attention.

BENEDICK: Still here, Miss Contempt? I'd quite forgotten you were still alive.

BEATRICE: How could Contempt die while there's so much about you to be contemptuous of? Even good manners would change to contempt when you appear.

BENEDICK: Then good manners are traitors. All women love me, except you. I wish I wasn't immune—I don't love anyone.

BEATRICE: Lucky for women that you don't! Otherwise they'd be pestered by a tedious lover. Thank God and my frigidity that

(Paraphrase continued on p. 63)

(Scene continued from p. 60)

cold blood I am of your humour for that. I had rather hear my dog bark at a crow than a man swear he loved me.

BENEDICK: God keep your ladyship still in that mind, so some gentleman or other shall scape a predestinate scratched face.

BEATRICE: Scratching could not make it worse and 'twere such a face as yours.

BENEDICK: Well, you are a rare parrot teacher.

BEATRICE: A bird of my tongue is better than a beast of yours.

BENEDICK: I would my horse had the speed of your tongue and so good a continuer. But keep your way, a God's name! I have done.

BEATRICE: You always end with a jade's** trick. I know you of old.

** A jade is a badly behaved horse.

(Paraphrase continued from p. 61)

I feel the same about men. I'd rather hear my dog barking at a crow than a man claiming he loved me.

BENEDICK: Let's hope God keeps you steadfast about that, so no lover inevitably gets his face scratched by your claws.

BEATRICE: Scratching wouldn't make him look any worse if he was as ugly as you.

BENEDICK: Can you only manage to repeat my words like a parrot?

BEATRICE: I'd rather talk like a bird than a beast...like you.

BENEDICK: I wish my horse galloped at the speed of your conversation and had your stamina. Carry on, for God's sake—I'm finished.

BEATRICE: You always refuse at the final fence. I'm familiar with your tricks.

You can see how Beatrice and Benedick capitalise on each other's ideas. It's rather like a relay race: one takes the baton of thought from the other and runs with it. Sometimes one will introduce a new baton of thought to see if the other is fast enough to grab it.

MUCH ADO ABOUT NOTHING
Act I, Scene 1
ANALYSIS OF REPARTEE

BEATRICE: I wonder that you will still be talking, Signior Benedick; nobody marks you.

Beatrice holds out the first baton by telling Benedick no one is paying any attention to what he is saying.

BENEDICK: What, my dear Lady Disdain! Are you yet living?

Benedick grabs the baton. "What" is the same insult turned onto Beatrice: he has paid so little attention to her, he didn't even realise she was there. He lays it on thicker by adding he didn't even realise she was still alive. This raises the stakes. He introduces a new baton by calling her Lady Disdain.

BEATRICE: Courtesy itself must convert to Disdain if you come in her presence.

Beatrice seizes on two elements in her reply: Lady Disdain and being alive. She says Disdain *thrives* on Benedick. She passes him a new baton of thought—that even courtesy would change into disdain when Benedick appeared.

BENEDICK: Then is courtesy a turncoat. But it is certain I am loved of all ladies, only you excepted; and I would I could find in my heart that I had not a hard heart; for truly I love none.

Benedick exploits the idea of such a total change of attitude by saying that courtesy would be a traitor to do that. The next baton he offers to Beatrice is that he doesn't love anyone.

BEATRICE: A dear happiness to women! They would else have been troubled with a pernicious suitor. I

> **thank God and my cold blood I am of your hu-
> mour for that. I had rather hear my dog bark at a
> crow than a man swear he loved me.**

Beatrice takes up that baton, doubled. The first riposte insults him
as a potential lover for any woman. The second congratulates herself for attributes not usually valued—she thanks God for her
frigidity and her indifference to wooing, because they make her as
immune to love as he is.

> BENEDICK: **God keep your ladyship still in that mind,
> so some gentleman or other shall scape a predes-
> tinate scratched face.**

Benedick picks up on her piety in invoking God and twists it
against her. May that same God that she invoked defend men
against her scratching claws. He manages an extra put-down about
the kind of lover she might expect "some gentleman *or other*."

> BEATRICE: **Scratching could not make it worse and
> 'twere such a face as yours.**

Beatrice, a bit on the ropes here, manages only a rather childish
come-back and makes the mistake of using the same word as
Benedick—scratching.

> BENEDICK: **Well, you are a rare parrot teacher.**

He accuses her of parroting him—just mimicking. And perhaps it's
a reference to her tone of voice as well?

> BEATRICE: **A bird of my tongue is better than a beast of
> yours.**

She transmutes the parrot idea to her own advantage. Her bird-
song is better than his bestial grunts.

> BENEDICK: **I would my horse had the speed of your
> tongue and so good a continuer. But keep your
> way, a God's name! I have done.**

Benedick sustains the animal idea by saying she's not so delicate—she's got the speed and stamina of a horse. He's had enough and now wants to go.

> BEATRICE: **You always end with a jade's trick. I know you of old.**

Beatrice has the final thrust. She builds on his mention of his horse; balking at further argument like that is behaving just like a horse refusing a fence. She's familiar with his tricks.

If you understand the structure of repartee, with practice your mind will work as swiftly as the characters'. It's a heady feeling to become as lethally quick as they are. The danger is that familiarity with the text will make you *too* swift. Doing all this homework can make you a touch complacent, and lead you into the false belief that once you've thought through every instant of these witty exchanges, that will inform your performance forever after. No such luck. You can never let up with the thought process and you must receive or extend each baton as if for the first time, every time. This means listening.

If you listen properly, without allowing your mind to rush ahead, and without distractions, then you will always have good timing. For example, Beatrice cannot leap in with a fast cue here:

> BENEDICK: **What, my dear Lady Disdain! Are you yet living?**

> BEATRICE: **Is it possible Disdain should die, while she hath such meet food to feed it as Signior Benedick?**

Why can't she? Because Benedick doesn't say the word "living" until the end of his line. She may pick up early on the idea of recycling "Disdain" in her reply, but she cannot balance his "living" with her idea about dying until she has heard his last syllable. It's a physiological fact that we breathe in when we have an *idea*—

even when we don't get to express it right away. Don't you remember having a great intake of breath in the classroom, when you shot your hand in the air, wanting to answer? "To inspire" is an old-fashioned word for to breathe. We inspire when we have an inspiration. If you don't anticipate, but allow your idea to form when you have heard enough data, then your breathing will assist your timing. You will never be artificially speedy; you will never tread on laughs. You will be able to pick up certain cues like lightning, well supported by breath, because you received all the information you needed to answer before the end of the other actor's line. (This can provide interesting reasons for not interrupting.) All of this matches an audience's rhythm of comprehension. You will never be too fast or too slow for them to understand repartee if you listen.

The last ingredient required is gusto. It's a great feeling to be good at a verbal game. Rap is good fun—so was repartee. Encourage Beatrice and Benedick to play the game of considering it merely an insult competition. They must trawl the text for digs at each other. The rest of the group is asked to applaud each successful dig. Score is kept for each character—Beatrice v. Benedick. The actors suddenly perceive a whole host of extra possibilities— for example, "I thank God" is one insult, "and my cold blood" (my frigidity) is another. With a slight separation and build, Beatrice can score two points instead of one. It slows down the scene of course, but this exercise is not about finesse, it's about *relish*. And it gives the actors a wonderful competitive edge. Placing the shot is crucial to high comedy. If one actor doesn't hit the ball fair and square to the other, then it's hard to return it. John Barton, the British director who has done wonderful work at the Royal Shakespeare Company, has a recurring plea to actors in rehearsal: "Serve it up, serve it up!"

Paraphrase, find the batons, work out the thought process that fuels your speech, listen, enjoy—that's repartee. Never drop the scene: keep the ball in the air by topping one another's tone. Use contrast, imitation, surprise, every device you can think of to take the other unawares. These things are independent of period and apply in any comedy.

✧ ✧ ✧

IRONY

Irony is another staple tool of wit in high comedy, and it often seems to come effortlessly to British actors because the British rarely say what they mean. "The speech we hear is an indication of what we don't hear ... One way of looking at speech is to say it is a constant stratagem to cover nakedness," says British playwright Harold Pinter. But I notice that some American actors (with the notable exception of New Yorkers!) are made uneasy by the notion that what they are saying is a decoy from the true intention, that the language distracts from what the character is actually thinking. They worry that the underlying meaning is not obvious enough, and in their attempts to communicate it they destroy all irony—because if it isn't delicate, it's not irony. It's nudge, nudge or worse.

Meaning one thing while saying something else is like singing a harmony with yourself, and the dominant tune is the spoken words. If they are convincing in their own right, and the audience realizes the unspoken irony a second later, it's funny. The character need not necessarily grasp the irony: awareness is not always part of the equation.

Another form of irony springs from the contradiction between words and actions. When this is deliberate it can be crude, such as "how very amusing" said with a straight face. Action should not reinforce an irony or it will overload it. For example, "I like you already more than I can say" should not be accompanied by a hostile stare. In fact, the action that accompanies irony should be ambiguously appropriate. In other words, it should be capable of being interpreted as the truth by the recipient, and recognizable as a cover-up by the audience. It's a fine line to tread.

Wilde's *The Importance of Being Earnest* is a minefield of irony, and the scene we are going to examine tips all too easily into leaden unfunniness if the actresses don't have a light touch. The question of style bedevils this play. "Is 'style' another word for 'stylisation'?" actors sometimes ask. No, it isn't, and that confusion is what has earned the word a bad name. The structure of Oscar Wilde's dialogue in *The Importance of Being Ernest*, and the formal gestures and movements that express it, are what some actors and directors take to be the style of the play. They are, of course, *part of the style*, but if one relies exclusively on form it should be no great surprise when the whole thing turns out to be a brittle bore. If the actors rely on the form to save them and don't dig below the surface, the play becomes an exercise in verbal and physical geometry. But if we look for the human and social drives that fuel the dialogue, then the play will have a life as well as a form.

By the time we encounter them in this scene from Act II, Cecily and Gwendolen are well established as a rural snob and an urban snob, with Cecily affecting innocence and Gwendolen sophistication. This, their first meeting, provokes a formal minuet of words that permits each to express her antagonistic feelings without losing the affectation she has adopted. Each is badly thrown by the appearance of the other—Cecily was expecting "one of the many good elderly women associated with Uncle Jack in his philanthropic work," and Gwendolen was *not* expecting a ravishing young girl in her fiance's country house! So before the first line of their scene together they have a mutual shock.

✧ ✧ ✧

THE IMPORTANCE OF BEING ERNEST
BY OSCAR WILDE

Act 2

CECILY: Pray let me introduce myself to you. My name is Cecily Cardew.

GWENDOLEN: Cecily Cardew? [*Moving to her and shaking hands.*] What a very sweet name! Something tells me we are going to be great friends. I like you already more than I can say. My first impressions of people are never wrong.

CECILY: How nice of you to like me so much after we have known each other such a comparatively short time. Pray sit down.

GWENDOLEN: [*Still standing up.*] I may call you Cecily, may I not?

CECILY: With pleasure!

GWENDOLEN: And you will always call me Gwendolen, won't you?

CECILY: If you wish.

GWENDOLEN: Then that is all quite settled, is it not?

CECILY: I hope so.

[*A pause—they both sit down together.*]

GWENDOLEN: Perhaps this might be a favourable opportunity for my mentioning who I am. My father is Lord Bracknell. You have never heard of papa I suppose?

CECILY: I don't think so.

GWENDOLEN: Outside the family circle, papa, I am glad to say, is entirely unknown. I think that is quite as it should be.

The home seems to me to be the proper sphere for the man. And certainly once a man begins to neglect his domestic duties he becomes painfully effeminate, does he not? And I don't like that. It makes men so very attractive. Cecily, mamma, whose views on education are remarkably strict, has brought me up to be extremely short sighted; it is part of her system; so do you mind my looking at you through my glasses?

CECILY: Oh! Not at all, Gwendolen. I am very fond of being looked at.

GWENDOLEN: [*After examining* CECILY *carefully through a lorgnette.*] You are here on a short visit, I suppose?

CECILY: Oh no! I live here.

GWENDOLEN: [*Severely.*] Really? Your mother, no doubt, or some female relative of advanced years resides here also?

CECILY: Oh no! I have no mother, nor, in fact any relations.

GWENDOLEN: Indeed?

CECILY: My dear guardian, with the assistance of Miss Prism, has the arduous task of looking after me.

GWENDOLEN: Your guardian?

CECILY: Yes, I am Mr. Worthing's ward.

GWENDOLEN: Oh! It is strange that he never mentioned to me that he had a ward. How secretive of him! He grows more interesting hourly. I am not sure, however, that the news inspires me with feelings of unmixed delight. [*Rising and going to her.*] I am very fond of you, Cecily; I have liked you ever since I met you! But I am bound to state that now that I know you are Mr. Worthing's ward, I cannot help expressing a wish you were—well, just a little older than you seem to be—and not quite so very alluring in appearance. In fact, if I may speak candidly—

CECILY: Pray do! I think that whenever one has anything unpleasant to say, one should always be quite candid.

GWENDOLEN: Well, to speak with perfect candour, Cecily, I wish that you were fully forty-two, and more than usually plain for your age. Ernest has a strong, upright nature. He is the very soul of truth and honor. Disloyalty would be as impossible to him as deception. But even men of the noblest possible moral character are extremely susceptible to the physical charms of others. Modern, no less than Ancient History supplies us with many most painful examples of what I refer to. If it were not so, indeed, History would be quite unreadable.

THE IMPORTANCE OF BEING ERNEST
Act 2
ANALYSIS

Let's analyze the opening of the scene before moving on to the irony, because the girls' methods of handling this skirmish differ radically:

> CECILY: **Pray let me introduce myself to you. My name is Cecily Cardew.**

Cecily's "Pray let me introduce myself" is not simply a social reflex but a cover-up for her shock at seeing Gwendolen.

> GWENDOLEN: **Cecily Cardew?** [*Moving to her and shaking hands.*] **What a very sweet name! Something tells me we are going to be great friends. I like you already more than I can say. My first impressions of people are never wrong.**

Gwendolen, while responding politely with a handshake, is moving immediately into townie gush intended to mask her true feelings. "What a very sweet name" is a patronising reaction to a name she probably regards as countrified and vulgarly alliterative. CC on the back of a hairbrush, for God's sake, one imagines her thinking. It is the "*very*" that gives her away, as do the overstatements of "*great* friends," "*more than I can say*." Try taking some of them out and see how the sincerity factor rises. There is an attempt to establish a hierarchy, too, because by moving straight into top gear and offering "great" friendship in the first moments of acquaintance, Gwendolen is showing that she is the one in control.

> CECILY: **How nice of you to like me so much after we have known each other such a comparatively short time. Pray sit down.**

Cecily is more than capable of parrying all this, and the difference in their armories immediately becomes apparent. For while Gwendolen resorts to saying the opposite of what she feels—except in her last remark, where for once text and irony collide—Cecily manages to convey her dislike without lying. Her irony comes from omission. Her method passes muster socially as perfect politeness—the sting is in the tail. Her first response to Gwendolen is successful on more than one level. She is parodying Gwendolen's superlatives with "so much" and "such." She is making it clear, with the use of "comparatively," that people usually like her pretty quickly anyway. There is an unspoken "oddly" before "nice"—or perhaps she has just omitted "if you were speaking the truth" from the end of the sentence. Compared to Gwendolen's effusions, she is sticking brilliantly close to the form of the truth. It would indeed be nice of Gwendolen to capitulate instantly to Cecily's charms *if* she had really done so.

> GWENDOLEN: [*Still standing up.*] I may call you Cecily, may I not?

Gwendolen wins the next flurry with a new weapon. She ignores Cecily's invitation to sit down. If she accepted she would be acknowledging Cecily's superior position as her hostess.

> CECILY: With pleasure!

> GWENDOLEN: And you will always call me Gwendolen, won't you?

Pressing on with the false intimacies, Gwendolen gives off another danger signal almost immediately. Once you'd started using someone's Christian name why on earth would you stop? Why does she need that qualifier, "always"? It's not just over the top, it opens up a whole new scenario. (I love these privileged glimpses into territory that's slightly off the map of the play, something that gives us a shaft of perception about the character's past. I call them "vistas.") The answer here, of course is that you'd stop using someone's Christian name, once you'd started, because you'd quarreled with them. Gwendolen, it's implied, has plenty of experience of this!

CECILY: **If you wish.**

GWENDOLEN: **Then that is all quite settled, is it not?**

CECILY: **I hope so.**

[*A pause—they both sit down together.*]

Cecily's cautious replies show she has perfectly understood Gwendolen's code. The reception of each other's veiled meanings is a crucial element in the timing—some codes will be cracked quicker than others. The girls reach a plateau at this point where both quite clearly recognize their mutual antagonism and realize that no-one is winning. There is a pause, dictated by Wilde, then they sit simultaneously, also dictated by Wilde. They are preparing for a second round. The rhythm of the scene is both physical and verbal, and it's very carefully plotted to reveal the psychology. It's not something imposed by actors or directors; it's already there.

✧ ✧ ✧

Now might be the moment to break off from analysis to discuss the problem of keeping the irony sufficiently delicate, because this little opening salvo between Gwendolen and Cecily is a perfect example of the words belying the the thoughts. The difficulty is not so much identifying what the irony or subtext is, although that is the first move, but of finding the *balance* between the top layer and the bottom. It's deeply boring if Gwendolen delivers her lines as if she doesn't mean them, semaphoring her true intentions to Cecily and the audience. Her chosen mask has to work effectively until later in the scene when truth and dialogue coincide because she can no longer keep up the pretence of politeness. All you have to do to achieve the required delicacy is identify the truth of the matter out loud *just once*. In rehearsal the actresses would say what they were feeling immediately before speaking their lines. It would sound something like this:

CECILY: <u>**Who on earth is this woman? Oh, I must re-**</u>

<u>member my manners.</u> **Pray let me introduce my-self to you. My name is Cecily Cardew.**

GWENDOLEN: <u>What the hell is a pretty girl doing here?</u> **Cecily Cardew?** <u>What a provincial sounding name.</u> [*Moving to her and shaking hands.*] **What a very sweet name!** <u>My hackles are up immediately.</u> **Some-thing tells me we are going to be great friends.** <u>I have taken an instinctive dislike to you.</u> **I like you already more than I can say. My first impressions of people are never wrong.**

CECILY: <u>Clearly you don't like me at all.</u> **How nice of you to like me so much after we have known each other such a comparatively short time.** <u>I'll show her who's mistress here.</u> **Pray sit down.**

GWENDOLEN: <u>I'll sit down when I want to, and not be-fore.</u> [*Still standing up.*] **I may call you Cecily, may I not?**

CECILY: <u>Since it pains you to say it.</u> **With pleasure!**

Having identified the irony in this way (and of course there are variations) the next step is to abandon it and trust the text. The mere fact that the actress has fully acknowledged the existence of the underlying meaning will forever color her delivery of the lines. You don't have to do any more. Say the lines as if you mean them. The irony you acknowledged in rehearsal will permeate your de-livery. The biggest danger is heavy handedness—look at me, I don't mean what I'm saying.

Sometimes it's hard to persuade actors that irony needs re-markably little assistance, and that they can use a completely truthful inflection without losing the discord between the words and what lies underneath. All they have to do is to *know* the truth. If you are finding this difficult, you might try an exercise I devised to persuade students of the power of the mind to transmit subtext. It's very simple, but it seems to work. In this scene, I would give Gwendolen and Cecily a handful of coins each. First I would ask them to play out the subtext, as in the preceding example. Then I would ask them to play the scene as if their lives depended upon their sincerity. But every time they felt that their thoughts diverged from the text, they could drop a coin. So the scene would play "What a very sweet name" (coin drop); "I like you already more than I can say" (coin drop); etc. Remarkably, the actresses come to trust the noise of the coin hitting the floor to do their work for them. They even start to drop each one in peculiarly expressive ways—a triumphant little tinkle, a bullet. What they gain is the courage not to *show* the underlying meaning with their voices or body language. Instead, they trust their brains, and Oscar Wilde, and the audience, and the irony is revealed in all its delicacy. The next step is to take the coins away!

> GWENDOLEN: **Perhaps this might be a favourable opportunity for my mentioning who I am. My father is Lord Bracknell. You have never heard of papa I suppose?**
>
> CECILY: **I don't think so.**
>
> GWENDOLEN: **Outside the family circle, papa, I am glad to say, is entirely unknown. I think that is quite as it should be. The home seems to me to be the proper sphere for the man. And certainly once a man begins to neglect his domestic duties he becomes painfully effeminate, does he not? And I don't like that. It makes men so very attractive. Cecily, mamma, whose views on education are remarkably strict, has brought me up to be extremely short sighted; it is part of her system; so do you mind my looking at you through my glasses?**

This being quite clearly the second round, Gwendolen changes the rhythm, and since she is a chip off the old block of her domineering mother, Lady Bracknell, she delivers a little lecture. It is on the subject of the position of the man in the family. Does she decide on the spot that it is better for the head of the family to be completely obscure, in order to gain back the point she lost by Cecily's ignorance of her father? Much of the comedy depends on Gwendolen being wrongfooted. At this early stage in the proceedings she is easily able to regain her balance. Her little homily is a big show-off. It's pyrotechnical, containing an elegant paradox (effeminacy making men so very attractive), and it displays her sophistication. She goes on at some length, partly because of her hereditary tendency to lecture, and partly because she wants to establish ascendancy over Cecily, but above all to make time to have a good look at her. What she sees is too flawless to be true, so she blows the whole elaborate manoeuvre that went before by asking if she may look closer through her spectacles! So the little homily is a cover for the true intention at the heart of the matter—can that skin texture be real?

> CECILY: **Oh! Not at all, Gwendolen. I am very fond of being looked at.**
>
> GWENDOLEN: [*After examining* CECILY *carefully through a lorgnette.*] **You are here on a short visit, I suppose?**
>
> CECILY: **Oh no! I live here.**
>
> GWENDOLEN: [*Severely.*] **Your mother, no doubt, or some female relative of advanced years resides here also?**
>
> CECILY: **Oh no! I have no mother, nor, in fact any relations.**
>
> GWENDOLEN: **Indeed?**
>
> CECILY: **My dear guardian, with the assistance of Miss Prism, has the arduous task of looking after me.**
>
> GWENDOLEN: **Your guardian?**
>
> CECILY: **Yes, I am Mr. Worthing's ward.**

Cecily's serene vanity plus the terrible visual confirmation of her perfection set Gwendolen back quite a bit. As a series of unpalatable facts are calmly established by Cecily, Gwendolen's mask slips further. "Severely" is Wilde's stage direction for Gwendolen's delivery, and certainly her fluency seems to have deserted her. Cecily is sufficiently in control to make a self-deprecating little joke about herself—"the arduous task of looking after me"—for of course she perceives herself as a model pupil. Gwendolen is sufficiently *out* of control to ignore this, impatiently fastening only on what interests her:

> **GWENDOLEN: Oh! It is strange that he never mentioned to me that he had a ward. How secretive of him! He grows more interesting hourly. I am not sure, however, that the news inspires me with feeling of unmixed delight. [*Rising and going to her.*] I am very fond of you, Cecily; I have liked you ever since I met you! But I am bound to state that now that I know you are Mr. Worthing's ward, I cannot help expressing a wish you were—well, just a little older than you seem to be—and not quite so very alluring in appearance. In fact, if I may speak candidly—**

This speech is a staircase of rising emotions. Gwendolen's gentility is definitely beginning to shred. Wilde has created an almost inescapable pattern of rhythms, provided not a syllable is skated over. "Oh!" is Gwendolen's shortest sentence to date. It certainly seems that the longer her sentences, the healthier her equilibrium. She has been knocked off her perch and the next few lines have to get her back on it again. She selects the word "strange" to give her time to calm down. "Strange" is a word without moral color—it doesn't tell us whether she approves or disapproves of Ernest concealing the existence of a ward. If she had said "odd" or "extraordinary" we would know where she stood. In comedic terms, an understated lingering on the word would indicate how carefully it had been chosen. So would an uncharacteristically long pause after "Oh!" while Gwendolen gathers her forces. As I've said elsewhere, a pause can be as long as you like, provided it is filled with mental activity, which gives it tension.

There are several ways of interpreting the next two lines—
"How secretive of him! He grows more interesting hourly." The
least likely is that Gwendolen means what she says. But perhaps
she is sufficiently at bay to respond genuinely on the first line,
condemning Ernest—and then, on reflection, in the second line,
is turned on by the idea of a complex, secretive fiance rather than
the conventional chap she thought she got engaged to. Or the first
sentence might pop out of her mouth before she could stop it, revealing far too much of her uneasy state of mind to Cecily. Then
the second line would be a cover-up. Secretiveness is fascinating to
sophisticated women like me, she might be saying to Cecily, using
another morally ambiguous word—"interesting"—to cover up her
feelings.

But she can't keep it up : "I am not sure, however, that the news
inspires me with unmixed delight." *Gwendolen speaks the truth!* It's
truth hedged about with a negative ("not sure") and qualifiers
("however," "unmixed"), truth grammatically constructed to sound
like its own opposite, but truth nevertheless.

She rises and goes to Cecily—Wilde's own stage directions.
This is the equivalent of the tanks going into action and there
should be a purposefulness to her movement at odds with her previous fashionable langour. She's not moving to make an effect or
to show off her pretty clothes, she's moving to make a primitive
statement: Stay Away From My Man. Her opening shots ("I am
very fond of you, Cecily; I have liked you ever since I met you")
show that she is perfectly in control and as gushing as ever, but like
her walk, her speech should lack the smooth ease of her early flat-
tery. For the first time the real feeling should sing through louder
than the gentility.

> CECILY: **Pray do! I think that whenever one has anything
> unpleasant to say, one should always be quite can-
> did.**
>
> GWENDOLEN: **Well, to speak with perfect candour,
> Cecily, I wish that you were fully forty-two, and**

more than usually plain for your age. Ernest has a strong, upright nature. He is the very soul of truth and honor. Disloyalty would be as impossible to him as deception. But even men of the noblest possible moral character are extremely susceptible to the physical charms of others. Modern, no less than Ancient History, supplies us with many most painful examples of what I refer to. If it were not so, indeed, History would be quite unreadable.

From here on the speech rolls on unstoppably. If anything, Cecily's vigorously frank interruption seems to lend energy to Gwendolen's outburst. A baton of candor is passed between them, growing in intensity as each uses it. It appears to me that the rhythm of Gwendolen's speeches seems to demand emphasis on the superfluous qualifying words; the words that are just there to make what she says even more excruciatingly polite and are one too many for any vestige of real politeness. For example, "*just* a little older than you seem to be, and not *quite* so very alluring in appearance"; "*perfect* candour"; "*fully* forty-two"; "*more* than usually plain." If you took away those emphatic words, Gwendolen would be almost straightforward. They are the clues which give her rage away and I think they should be relished, for Gwendolen is definitely out of control. But don't forget the corset of formal manners that is ever present, or the fact that there is a long way to go in the insult game that is played out between these two in the rest of this scene.

4

CHARACTER

I wish I could offer you some foolproof working method that would always reward you with a fully rounded character. There are safety nets and there are methods of exploration, but despite such authoritative sounding titles as Stanislavsky's *Building a Character*, no single process works for everyone. The most accessible and reliable part takes place before rehearsal: background research, collecting and reacting to the stimuli that seem relevant (in an abstract way) such as music, novels, paintings. In this golden period almost everything seems to connect with one's explorations. But what does one actually begin with on the first day of rehearsal? Usually the firm conviction that one is invisible. Flesh and blood and intelligence and research seem to count for nothing. I tell actors that they *do* exist and that they do not need to discard themselves as a starting point. Don't panic and start looking for a change of personality—allow your evolution to occur organically. This is a process that cannot be hurried and does not necessarily demand a zombie-like clean slate.

Searching for a character is, or should be, a free, enjoyable creative process. The actor is the missing link between text and performance. The playwright expects us to join up the dots in a new way—what else can we do? It's not a tidy process, it's an anarchic one, but for some reason we resist acknowledging this. There are some ideas and triggers that have helped me. They are not presented here in any particular order: I never needed them in the same order twice, nor at any particular stage in the process, because believing in one's own reality is a cumulative process that is different for every play. Day by day in rehearsal we add pieces of our character that convince us at a visceral level. There are frequent failures. It is to Stanislavsky that we owe the best description of the safety net for the imagination: "the magical, the creative *if*... the imagined truth which the actor can believe as sincerely and with greater enthusiasm than he believes practical truth, just as the child believes in the existence of its doll and of all life in and around it. From the moment of the appearance of the *if*, the actor passes from the plane of actual reality into the plane of another life..."

If I were this person, what would I do? "Do" is the key word. Character is what we do, how we do it, and why we do it. What you do reveals who you are. The selection of actions is as important as the dialogue, and without that selection dialogue is empty even in high comedy. This doesn't presume busyness, or a lot of stage business, but a subtle underpinning of thought with body language. For example, Mirabell and Millamant can't touch each other amorously because it would be beyond the bounds of decorum, but their repressed passion can express itself in other ways: Millamant could stroke the material of her dress or the cover of her book unconsciously, as she's unable to stroke anything else. The sight of it could paralyze Mirabell—he could be unable to move until she stops, or lose the thread of his argument.

Character is never simple, and almost always works on more than one level. Consider your character at his most honest, as he is in soliloquy or alone. Consider him at ease with his family and trusted intimates. Then consider him at large in the world, impressing himself on strangers. In life you sometimes try to project an image of yourself that is at odds with the truth: so too, very probably, does your character. What are your character's hypocrisies? Acknowledge how differently *you* would behave sitting next to different types in an aeroplane—your mother, a film star, a Sri Lankan woman returning home. Our need at the time governs our behaviour, and our need as characters is usually for some sort of reward that reflects the world of the play. The act is for the other characters, not for the audience. The audience will always see through the pretence, the other characters may not.

The performances I have most enjoyed have contained fresh, original ideas, expressed both physically and in line readings. What we're looking for is your unique expression of a role, your unique insight. Cliches spring to mind with terrifying ease, so choose a quirky route. Presumably you are familiar with everything the play reveals about your character: if there is a choice, go for the interesting and unusual one. We tend, having done our homework, to balance the clues to character that we find in a play against what we know to be true of human nature. This is fine, as far as it goes. But the more we know of human nature, the more we come to realize that lack of consistency is a distinguishing human characteristic.

Actors torment themselves needlessly trying to find consistency in a character. For example, what if Mirabell's saucy reply, "Then I'll get up in the morning as early as I please" is not a swift, jousting, sexy tease, but a recovery. Suppose his voice might betray his passion—Millamant' last remarks are very provocative—so he has to take a pause and swallow. Suppose his reply, when he was able to make it, is hoarse with the idea of really making love to her, and instead of seeing the assured man of the world we have come to expect, we see how desperately he wants her. All much more interesting than clipped repartee, isn't it? And imagine the split-second pause afterwards while Millamant contemplates the same pleasure and then makes *her* recovery...Michael Redgrave, an English actor who never took the obvious route, said that "the abiding necessity for every actor, as for every artist, is the avoidance of cliche, the easy, effective, conventional mode or trick of self-expression. Cliche is like a weed: no garden is free from it all the time. The greatest performances are those which are most free from it, those in which every detail has been freshly conceived and which retains at each performance enough of that freshness."

Sometimes one must find the courage to start again, even dangerously late in the proceedings. The overriding fear is that nothing one has done is of any use, that none of the hard-won data will serve. What actually happens, however, is that the data re-arranges itself in an instant, provided you find the switch for the current.

Never act alone. You can't play qualities, you can only bounce them off the other characters. Faulkland doesn't play jealousy, he plays incredulity at Julia's lack of understanding of it. In that case, she actually does what his characterization requires by not understanding. It doesn't matter if the other characters don't in fact come up with what your character needs, though; the point is that your character *perceives* the quality that justifies his own attitudes. For example, if you are playing a humble person, then find the others intimidatingly attractive and intelligent. If you are playing someone who is vain, then decide the rest are plain and dull and frightfully impressed with you. When you try this, don't consciously change the mechanics of your delivery, just allow the others to take on these characteristics *in your mind*.

These next suggestions are for when you're in trouble; they come from a structural perspective and I have found that they can reveal something one has missed:

1. Is it your function in the play to contrast with another character? Contrasted attitudes are comic and playwrights often use this device. Be aware of its potential.

2. Are you part of a double-act? If you are half of a comic pairing, perhaps the other character takes responsibility for an aspect of self you are struggling, and failing, to provide?

3. Ask yourself, what is the drama? In other words, what is the conflict, the opposing force without which your character would proceed without hindrance? If you are proceeding without hindrance, you are probably proceeding undramatically. Look for the obstacles.

And this is an exercise that has saved me more than once:

4. Choose a key line or short speech of your character, one that seems to you to encapsulate him or her. Tell the rest of the company what the line is and ask them to cross the room, one by one, repeating that line continuously as a physical and verbal cartoon of what they see in your character. Have them queue up, then, in swift succession, walk or hop or shuffle or mince across the rehearsal room, repeating the line as many times as it takes to cross it. You will get a number of exaggerated lightning character sketches—some of them revealing aspects of your character you never perceived. It can be cruel, because it can unwittingly reveal one's own inadequacies when another actor cuts right to the heart of the character, but it's nearly always very helpful.

Henri Bergson pointed out in his theory of comedy that rigidity of mind or body is what begets comedy. Look for what is inflexible in your character, what automatic response he or she cannot help giving if the right buttons are pushed. "The comic is that side of a person which reveals his likeness to a thing, that aspect of human events which, through its peculiar inelasticity, conveys the impression of pure mechanism, of automatism, of movement without life." In other words, look for habit as a character essential. Faulkland and Julia in *The Rivals* are trapped by their own pretensions about their romance. An inflated idea of love demands romantic pomposity, and their habit is to adopt a special high-toned language when they talk to, or even about, each other. It is a reflex that is extremely comic, a *folie a deux* to aggrandise their relationship.

A great part of the comedy of the characters in the following extract from Noel Coward's *Private Lives* lies in the predictability of their responses: they know how to push each other's buttons. We seem to dislike the idea that the clever sophisticates who populate high comedy have a coarser side. But they do. Manners are learned, they are not instinctive, and you will learn them in order to play a part. But underneath the manners is the naked self and the opportunities a play gives us to display it must be seized. It's a great shame if the actress playing Amanda in *Private Lives* becomes so absorbed with her portrayal of minx-like elegance that she misses the pure, raw fishwife just below the surface. Coward has supplied the latter too—and the juxtaposition of smooth and coarse enhances the comedy of both.

American actors often ask me if I want them to assume an accent to play certain high comedies. Not necessarily, and not if it creates difficulties. If you're wrestling with an accent you may not be able to communicate much else. Be consistent, that's all. There's nothing worse than hearing an accent roam continents. Seventeenth-century speech in England didn't sound at all like modern English, so don't be daunted by the early plays. Comedy is nearly always extinguished by visible effort, so use standard American or find a comfortable equivalent American accent. A Southern belle of a Millamant in *The Way of the World*, or a Bostonian Amanda in *Private Lives*, would preserve class and caprice far better than tortured vowels.

Private Lives is a play in which absolutely nothing happens, in plot terms, after the first act. Two couples are on honeymoon in a hotel in the south of France. We meet each couple in turn as they come out on their adjoining balconies. Sybil, a young and rather silly girl, is married to Elyot, a sophisticated and amusing man. Amanda, a witty, volatile femme fatale, is married to the hearty, earnest, brainless Victor. Both Elyot and Amanda have been married before, to each other. In a deservedly classic scene they discover each other, have a short, sharp row, after which they realise they can't live without each other and run away together, abandoning their new spouses.

The whole story has been told by the time we find Amanda and Elyot in Act II in her flat in Paris, where they make love and argue, for the entire act.

Amanda and Elyot are part of a long tradition that includes

Beatrice and Benedick, and Mirabell and Millamant, in which the protagonists are evenly matched and at times almost indistinguishable. This is not the comedy of contrast but the comedy of double-act. I remember when I was rehearsing the part of Amanda for a production that ran a year in the West End that at some point in that middle act Elyot and I started saying each other's lines. We realized the mistake, of course, but it seemed worth pursuing, and the curious thing was that apart from a bit of gender confusion in the references to off-stage lovers, none of it felt out of character at all. I don't think Coward differentiated much between them on a gender basis. Certainly many applications have been made to the Coward Estate to do all-male productions, but this interesting variation has not yet been permitted.

The extract I have chosen is a sequence of rows and reconciliations, so it's like climbing a staircase with rests on the landings. Just before we start here, Elyot and Amanda have reached the calmest plateau in the play, and the most serious. Their attitudes to the topics of love and death and separation are cloaked in their usual flippancy, but an extremely touching subtext of tenderness and intimacy comes singing through despite the jokes. That is the mood at the start here, but after the mention of Peter Burden the momentum of combat never falters. There are no more landings or plateaus. The sequence of rows goes on relentlessly until they attack each other physically. There are changes of tempo, but any "rests" are merely panting pauses on a staircase of growing animosity.

I should explain to anyone who doesn't know the play that The Row is central to Elyot and Amanda's relationship. They can't live without each other, but they certainly can't live *with* each other, so they devise a method of stopping their rows from spiralling into physical violence. Whoever is most in control shouts "Solomon Isaacs" to break the mood and signify a truce. In extreme cases—and we see plenty of those earlier in Act II—it gets truncated to "Sollocks."

PRIVATE LIVES

BY NOEL COWARD

Act II

ELYOT: Do you remember that awful scene we had in Venice?

AMANDA: Which particular one?

ELYOT: The one when you bought that little painted wooden snake on the Piazza, and put it on my bed.

AMANDA: Oh, Charles. That was his name, Charles. He did wriggle so beautifully.

ELYOT: Horrible thing, I hated it.

AMANDA: Yes, I know you did. You threw it out of the window into the Grand Canal. I don't think I'll ever forgive you for that.

ELYOT: How long did the row last?

AMANDA: It went on intermittently for days.

ELYOT: The worst one was in Cannes when your curling irons burnt a hole in my new dressing gown. [*He laughs.*]

AMANDA: It burnt my comb too, and all the towels in the bathroom.

ELYOT: That was a rouser, wasn't it?

AMANDA: That was the first time you ever hit me.

ELYOT: I didn't hit you very hard.

AMANDA: The manager came in and found us rolling on the floor, biting and scratching like panthers. Oh dear, oh dear—[*She laughs helplessly.*]

ELYOT: I shall never forget his face. [*They both collapse with laughter.*]

AMANDA: How ridiculous, how utterly, utterly ridiculous.

ELYOT: We were very much younger then.

AMANDA: And very much sillier.

ELYOT: As a matter of fact the real cause of that row was Peter Burden.

AMANDA: You knew there was nothing in that.

ELYOT: I didn't know any thing of the sort, you took presents from him.

AMANDA: Presents: only a trivial little brooch.

ELYOT: I remember it well, bristling with diamonds. In the worst possible taste.

AMANDA: Not at all, it was very pretty. I still have it and I wear it often.

ELYOT: You went out of your way to torture me over Peter Burden.

AMANDA: No, I didn't, you worked the whole thing up in your jealous imagination.

ELYOT: You must admit that he was in love with you, wasn't he?

AMANDA: Just a little, perhaps. Nothing serious.

ELYOT: You let him kiss you. You said you did.

AMANDA: Well, what of it?

ELYOT: What of it?

AMANDA: It gave him a lot of pleasure, and it didn't hurt me.

ELYOT: What about me?

AMANDA: If you hadn't been so suspicious and nosey you'd never have known a thing about it.

ELYOT: That's a nice point of view, I must say.

AMANDA: Oh dear, I'm bored with this conversation.

ELYOT: So am I, bored stiff. [*He goes over to the table.*] Want some brandy?

AMANDA: No thanks.

ELYOT: I'll have a little, I think.

AMANDA: I don't see why you want it, you've already had two glasses.

ELYOT: No particular reason, anyhow they were very small ones.

AMANDA: It seems so silly to go on, and on, and on with a thing.

ELYOT: [*Pouring himself a glass.*] You can hardly call three liqueur glasses in a whole evening going on, and on, and on.

AMANDA: It's become a habit with you.

ELYOT: You needn't be so grand, just because you don't happen to want any yourself at the moment.

AMANDA: Don't be so stupid.

ELYOT: [*Irritably.*] Really Amanda—

AMANDA: What?

ELYOT: Nothing.

> [AMANDA *sits down on the sofa, and, taking small mirror from her bag, gazes at her face critically, and then uses some lipstick and powder.*]

ELYOT: [*A trifle nastily.*] Going out somewhere, dear?

AMANDA: No, just making myself fascinating for you.

ELYOT: That reply has broken my heart.

AMANDA: The woman's job is to allure the man. Watch me a minute will you?

ELYOT: As a matter of fact that's perfectly true.

AMANDA: Oh, no it isn't.

ELYOT: Yes it is.

AMANDA: No it isn't.

ELYOT: Yes it is.

AMANDA: [*Snappily.*] Oh be quiet.

ELYOT: It's a pity you didn't have any more brandy; it might have made you a little less disagreeable.

AMANDA: It doesn't seem to have worked such wonders with you.

ELYOT: Snap, snap, snap; like a little adder.

AMANDA: Adders don't snap, they sting.

ELYOT: Nonsense, they have a little bag of venom behind their fangs and they snap.

AMANDA: They sting.

ELYOT: They snap.

AMANDA: I don't care, do you understand? I don't care. I don't mind if they bark and roll around like hoops.

ELYOT: [*After a slight pause.*] Did you see much of Peter Burden after our divorce?

AMANDA: Yes, I did, quite a lot.

ELYOT: I suppose you let him kiss you a good deal more then.

AMANDA: Mind your own business.

ELYOT: You must have had a riotous time.

[AMANDA *doesn't answer, so he stalks about the room.*]

ELYOT: No restraint at all—very enjoyable—you never had much anyhow.

AMANDA: You're quite insufferable; I expect it's because you're drunk.

ELYOT: I'm not in the least drunk.

AMANDA: You always had a weak head.

ELYOT: I think I mentioned once before that I have only had three minute liqueur glasses of brandy the whole evening long. A child of two couldn't get drunk on that.

AMANDA: On the contrary, a child of two could get violently drunk on only one glass of brandy.

ELYOT: Very interesting. How about a child of four and a child of six and a child of nine?

AMANDA: [*Turning her head away.*] Oh do shut up.

ELYOT: [*Witheringly.*]: We might get up a splendid little debate about that, you know, Intemperate Tots.

AMANDA: Not very funny dear; you'd better have some more brandy.

ELYOT: Very good idea, I will. [*He pours out another glass and gulps it defiantly.*]

AMANDA: Ridiculous ass.

ELYOT: I beg your pardon?

AMANDA: I said ridiculous ass!

ELYOT: [*With great dignity.*] Thank you.

PRIVATE LIVES
Act II
ANALYSIS OF SCENE

ELYOT: Do you remember that awful scene we had in Venice?

AMANDA: Which particular one?

ELYOT: The one when you bought that little painted wooden snake on the Piazza, and put it on my bed.

AMANDA: Oh, Charles. That was his name, Charles. He did wriggle so beautifully.

ELYOT: Horrible thing, I hated it.

AMANDA: Yes, I know you did. You threw it out of the window into the Grand Canal. I don't think I'll ever forgive you for that.

ELYOT: How long did the row last?

AMANDA: It went on intermittently for days.

ELYOT: The worst one was in Cannes when your curling irons burnt a hole in my new dressing gown. [*He laughs.*]

AMANDA: It burnt my comb too, and all the towels in the bathroom.

ELYOT: That was a rouser, wasn't it?

AMANDA: That was the first time you ever hit me.

ELYOT: I didn't hit you very hard.

AMANDA: The manager came in and found us rolling on the floor, biting and scratching like panthers. Oh dear, oh dear— [*She laughs helplessly.*]

ELYOT: I shall never forget his face.

[*They both collapse with laughter.*]

AMANDA: How ridiculous, how utterly, utterly ridiculous.

The mood at the start of this section—just before they speak—is a slightly melancholy intimacy, a hangover from the serious discussion just before. So find a physical way of expressing the fact that they are relaxed and united. Maybe they are both on the floor, maybe he has his head in her lap?

On the face of it, bringing up the subject of an old row might seem provocative. But in the world of Amanda and Elyot rows are evidence of passion, so this segues naturally from the last topic. But as they get in to detailed reminiscence about "rows we have known" we see that they are like collectors of Ming vases identifying prize specimens. Don't fall into the trap of under-energizing because you are talking about something in the past. When obsessionalists reminisce about the objects of their obsession, they get worked up all over again. When my grandmother told me how naughty my mother was as a little girl, she would get angry with her all over again, forty years later. Something of the passion of the past event must infuse the present description of it. Bring it into the "now." And ask why your character is talking about this at that particular moment—the "why" is in the now too. Perhaps Elyot is trying to break the mood of melancholy by bringing up a riproaring past row. The point is that Amanda is caught up by the memory into recreating something of the hectic mood of the rows themselves; she is not bogged down by fond nostalgia, but energized by it.

The way that they laugh gives us a clue to the physical abandon of those rows. These people are creatures of extremes. You can't play this scene with a little prissy giggling. Laughing to order can be tough, and one of the ways to help its spontaneity is to suppress it. Then it can bubble up like a spring at the appropriate moment. There are seven lines of memories of the row in Cannes, and Coward has given a stage direction that Elyot should laugh at his first mention of it. So he can be fighting off mirth until it engulfs him after the memory of the manager's face. Try playing this first section as if you were children in a nursery, tickling each other. You will retain the sensation of ecstatic memory long after you have stopped tickling! The childish values of Amanda and Elyot are apparent here. They caused some damage to the hotel and each other and shocked the manager, and they remember the episode with enormous fondness. If you want a substitution, it's like pop-stars wrecking their hotel suite—absolutely conscience-less destruction because they can pay.

There's a chance here to avoid a cliched approach to character. In any other play, the line, "That was the first time you ever hit me" would be accusatory. But for Amanda it might well be a sentimental memory. She might be glorying in it, whimsically—"That was the first time I goaded you sufficiently to break that old taboo." It seems perfectly plausible to me that Amanda would take an unconventional moral tack and fondly remember the first slap, the first punch and the first time he threw a chair at her, say.

> ELYOT: **We were very much younger then.**
>
> AMANDA: **And very much sillier.**
>
> ELYOT: **As a matter of fact the real cause of that row was Peter Burden.**
>
> AMANDA: **You knew there was nothing in that.**

Here's a beautiful example of a behavioral irony, of the body contradicting the words. Having behaved like three-year-olds, rolling about on the floor with glee at their own bad behavior in Cannes, he says they were younger *then* and she says they were sillier *then*. Of course, they've been behaving childishly and stupidly before our very eyes. And, naturally, if the actors aren't apparently oblivious to the irony, there won't be any.

After all that immoderate laughter, there is a landing or a plateau just before Elyot floats the idea of Peter Burden being the cause. They need a pause to recover. You can go anywhere emotionally after a big bout of laughter, up or down, but two people will not necessarily move in the same direction. Elyot and Amanda's moods are not connected here—one is thinking about Peter Burden, the other isn't. It's very interesting on stage to see moods diverging, to see someone's surprise (sometimes displeasure) when they realize the direction in which the other person's thoughts have gone. Amanda might still be in the aftermath of laughter, a sort of limbo, while Elyot remembers Peter Burden's role. It might be that Elyot introduces the topic of Peter Burden quite unaggressively. He doesn't expect to start a row. He thinks that as they have been reminiscing harmlessly about fights, he can wave this red rag to himself, the bull, and it won't affect him at all. We all raise painful subjects quite calmly at times, in the belief that we can handle them without getting upset, and it turns out we're not capable of it at all. But Elyot's jealousy is at a low level here and well disguised.

It doesn't fool Amanda, however. Peter Burden is such a familiar old danger signal. How do we know she is alerted? By a ping, that pause with a sting in it. Maybe she stops mid-movement, perhaps while straightening her clothes after the laughing, or while running her fingers through her hair. If movement is arrested in a mercurial creature like this, it tells us a lot. Maybe she is elaborately casual in her reply, hoping to avert any more Peter Burden discussion. Maybe she is genuinely incredulous. Maybe she is exhausted at the prospect of going over all this yet again. When in doubt with Coward, bleach out the tone and let the words do the work—sometimes his intentions become clearer that way.

> ELYOT: **I didn't know anything of the sort, you took presents from him.**
>
> AMANDA: **Presents: only a trivial little brooch.**
>
> ELYOT: **I remember it well, bristling with diamonds. In the worst possible taste.**
>
> AMANDA: **Not at all, it was very pretty. I still have it and I wear it often.**
>
> ELYOT: **You went out of your way to torture me over Peter Burden.**
>
> AMANDA: **No, I didn't, you worked the whole thing up in your jealous imagination.**

ELYOT: **You must admit that he was in love with you, wasn't he?**

AMANDA: **Just a little, perhaps. Nothing serious.**

Elyot never gives up, he doggedly pursues his own line of reasoning. But he is dealing with a phenomenon of illogicality in Amanda. One of her most dominant characteristics is a capacity to distort logic with such certainty that the most ludicrous statements appear, for an instant, to be true. For example, she echoes the word "presents" so incredulously that for a moment we accept the possibilty that a brooch is *not* a present.

What a pejorative verb "bristling" is when taken in conjunction with diamonds! "Tastefully studded with" would be what a jeweller would say. Taste is something these two value more than almost anything—it's one of their absolutes. Accepting rich gifts is nothing compared to the immoral mistake of wearing a vulgar brooch.

Amanda, wounded, responds with a three-beat mugging. She says (1.) it's *very* pretty (he had taste) (2.) I *still* have it (I kept it because I have fond memories of him) (3.) I wear it *often* (I publically display evidence of that relationship). I see a parallel with Millamant's three-beat capitulation to Mirabell: "I may/by degrees/dwindle into a wife." They're different weapons, but they're out of the same arsenal.

Elyot continues to behave as he must have done when this actually happened. The shift from past to present that I keep urging on you is here perfectly demonstrated. They are never far apart in scenes of reminiscence. Both Elyot and Amanda are equally irritated by this topic, she because he behaved (and is behaving) like a jealous bull, he because she betrayed him and is unrepentant. He is quite openly wounded and quite openly aggressive. She is contemptuous of him for bringing the matter up but her lofty tone covers an increasing fury. From this point on, although each adopts different devices—sarcasm, violent contradiction, contempt—their interior tension never slackens. There are no more plateaus.

ELYOT: **You let him kiss you. You said you did.**

AMANDA: **Well, what of it?**

ELYOT: **What of it?**

AMANDA: **It gave him a lot of pleasure, and it didn't hurt me.**

ELYOT: **What about me?**

AMANDA: **If you hadn't been so suspicious and nosey you'd never have known a thing about it.**

ELYOT: **That's a nice point of view, I must say.**

Why does Elyot add "You said you did"? She wouldn't bother to deny it. It's because she doesn't respond *at all* to his accusation. And when she does answer it's not remotely what he requires—it's "so I did, so what?" He's incredulous. She baits him with one of her special pieces of logic, which makes him pathetically indignant—"What about me?" His sophistication has evaporated, which shows just how much he cares. She tops her own wacky logic with the ultimate shift of blame: "If you hadn't been so suspicious and nosey, you wouldn't have known a thing about it." She makes her infidelity his fault! I'm reminded of *The Way of the World* again, when Mirabell says he doesn't want a wife who goes off to the theatre with another man, and then comes home and blames *him*. There are certain constants in the relationships between high comedy heroes and heroines.

Such a wild piece of logic might give even Elyot, who is used to these displays, a moment's pause. He can't complain about her point of view until its full, mad import has sunk in. It's a baton of thought, and he can't pick it up until he's ready. It's very easy in this play to get carried away by the speed of their responses and pick up cues faster than thought.

AMANDA: **Oh dear, I'm bored with this conversation.**

ELYOT: **So am I, bored stiff.** [*He goes over to the table.*] **Want some brandy?**

AMANDA: **No thanks.**

ELYOT: **I'll have a little, I think.**

AMANDA: **I don't see why you want it, you've already had two glasses.**

ELYOT: **No particular reason, anyhow they were very small ones**

AMANDA: **It seems so silly to go on, and on, and on with a thing.**

ELYOT: [*Pouring himself a glass.*] **You can hardly call three liqueur glasses in a whole evening going on, and on, and on.**

AMANDA: **It's become a habit with you.**

ELYOT: **You needn't be so grand, just because you don't happen to want any yourself at the moment.**

AMANDA: **Don't be so stupid.**

ELYOT: [*Irritably.*] **Really Amanda—**

AMANDA: **What?**

ELYOT: **Nothing.**

Once her logic has been challenged, Amanda doesn't want to play any more. (If you're going to criticize my methods, let's stop.)

I think Elyot is offering an olive branch when he offers her a drink, and right up until the moment she accuses him of having a habit, he is fighting his own irritation and struggling to be reasonable. She, on the other hand, is being deliberately provocative. That one little "no thanks" gives us a vista of her life with an alcoholic—she's using that critical, martyred tone of the wife who isn't going to drink and doesn't think that he should either. (We've seen her knock back countless cocktails with breezy relish.) His reasonableness and her jabbing should be swung into with the familiarity of a dance—and, of course, when someone else's attack or defence strategy is familiar to us, it's even more maddening. Everything each one says is meant to be the closer, the knock-out, so each continuation winds the other one up still further. One way to catch the tone is to say "and *that's* the end of it" at the end of each line. You'll see how quickly things escalate. Coward gives onamatopoeic presents as Congreve does: here his "on and on and on" is a gift to both parties.

Elyot obviously hits home when he points out, with perfectly justification, that she normally drinks just as much as he does. As the fishwife side of Amanda emerges, the sophistication of her dialogue declines. We knew that Gwendolen was on the ropes when her sentences got shorter. We know Amanda is in trouble when she gets childishly abusive. "Don't be so stupid" is not much of a comeback, but the tone must be very aggressive. Similarly, her "What?" must be sufficiently awe-inspiring to end round one. There's an implicit "fight me, come on, fight me, baby, if you dare," and he decides not to pursue it.

> [AMANDA *sits down on the sofa, and taking a small mirror from her bag, gazes at ther face critically, and then uses some lipstick and powder.*]
>
> ELYOT: [*A trifle nastily.*] Going out somewhere dear?
>
> AMANDA: No, just making myself fascinating for you.
>
> ELYOT: That reply has broken my heart.
>
> AMANDA: The woman's job is to allure the man. Watch me a minute will you?
>
> ELYOT: As a matter of fact that's perfectly true.
>
> AMANDA: Oh, no it isn't.
>
> ELYOT: Yes it is.
>
> AMANDA: No it isn't.
>
> ELYOT: Yes it is.
>
> AMANDA: [*Snappily.*] Oh be quiet.
>
> ELYOT: It's a pity you didn't have any more brandy; it might have made you a little less disagreeable.

AMANDA: **It doesn't seem to have worked such wonders with you.**

ELYOT: **Snap, snap, snap; like a little adder.**

AMANDA: **Adders don't snap, they sting.**

ELYOT: **Nonsense, they have a little bag of venom behind their fangs and they snap.**

AMANDA: **They sting.**

ELYOT: **They snap.**

AMANDA: **I don't care, do you understand? I don't care. I don't mind if they bark and roll around like hoops.**

If cosmetics can be applied in a manner calculated to annoy, then that is what Amanda is doing. It is a parody of making herself beautiful, like the wicked queen in *Snow White*. When she says she is making herself fascinating for him, she is mocking the woman's magazine concept of making your face pretty for your man, putting on a nice frilly frock and welcoming him home to a candlelight supper. Said dead-pan, with a tiny emphasis on "fascinating," it's an incredibly cutting line, because it makes fun of his expectations of women. Of course, they *aren't* his expectations, but he cleverly adopts them on the spot to annoy her further, driving her to one of her aggressive full stops—"Oh, be quiet".

While the sophistication of Amanda's vocabulary occasionally declines, I don't think diction ever deserts either of them, as is evidenced by the war of the consonants which takes place here. Actually, it's a war which takes place in the playground—snap, sting, snap, sting—and is ended by one child metaphorically kicking the other in the shins and running away—"I don't care, I don't care." Amanda goes into the stratosphere with this piece of mad zoological invention, and having hit the heights with "hoops" may well be left feeling slightly stupid, particularly if Elyot uses part of the subsequent pause to let her dangle, hoist with her own petard.

ELYOT: [*After a slight pause.*] **Did you see much of Peter Burden after our divorce?**

AMANDA: Yes, I did, quite a lot.

ELYOT: I suppose you let him kiss you a good deal more then.

AMANDA: Mind your own business.

ELYOT: You must have had a riotous time.

[AMANDA *doesn't answer, so he stalks about the room.*]

ELYOT: No restraint at all—very enjoyable—you never had much anyhow.

AMANDA: You're quite insufferable; I expect it's because you're drunk.

ELYOT: I'm not in the least drunk.

AMANDA: You always had a weak head.

ELYOT: I think I mentioned once before that I have only had three minute liqueur glasses of brandy the whole evening long. A child of two couldn't get drunk on that.

AMANDA: On the contrary, a child of two could get violently drunk on only one glass of brandy.

ELYOT: Very interesting. How about a child of four and a child of six and a child of nine?

AMANDA: [*Turning her head away.*] Oh do shut up.

ELYOT: [*Witheringly.*] We might get up a splendid little debate about that, you know, Intemperate Tots.

AMANDA: Not very funny dear; you'd better have some more brandy.

ELYOT: Very good idea, I will. [*He pours out another glass and gulps it defiantly.*]

AMANDA: Ridiculous ass.

ELYOT: I beg your pardon?

AMANDA: I said ridiculous ass!

ELYOT: [*With great dignity.*] Thank you.

Out of the pause comes the specter of Peter Burden, a specter we realize has never left Elyot. Amanda and Elyot swing into the familiar routines, Burden first, drink second, their blood pressure rising with each exchange. They rip through their repertoire of disguises for naked rage—contempt: "You always had a weak head"; condescension: "I *think* I mentioned once before"; superiority: "On the contrary"; elaborate irony "*Very* interesting"; and so on. They pick up each others' tone: "You are so stupid"—"NO, dear, *you* are so stupid." But whatever the mechanism, they are on an ascending gradient. "Ridiculous ass" is not inaudible the first time, it is simply served up in a way that demands a repeat. It is slyly insulting, a snigger behind the hand that is meant to be seen. It also requires elaborate articulation, which Amanda would not neglect in her second rendition.

We leave them cranking up for another round of subtle and not so subtle torments, a failed Sollocks, and physical violence. The third act is more of the same, conducted in front of Victor and Sybil, who catch the infection themselves and quarrel the curtain down, while Amanda and Elyot steal away to fight another day.

5

SLALOM

I've chosen the following scene from *The Rivals* because the character of Faulkland provides a classic example of volatility of mood. Faulkland's emotions are as real and as serious to him as any in tragedy: any attempt by the actor to dilute them "because it's comedy" would be fatal. It's not any lack of intensity that makes Faulkland's feelings funny. It's the speed and suddenness with which his emotions come and go that make us realize they are trivial and therefore funny. I call the negotiation of these swiftly changing moods *slalom*, because, just as in the ski event, we need to chart a course and then execute multiple turns at speed.

The first problem of the high comedy slalom is to identify each change of feeling and to occupy each moment of that feeling to the hilt. The second problem is moving cleanly from one emotion to the next. If there is any seepage, if the change is not made absolutely surgically, then the whole sequence becomes a blur. The process of change must not show, only the juxtaposition of one mood against the next. The final problem is to get the changes up to speed while preserving both the extremes of feeling and the clarity. You have to pull the rug out from under one emotion, as it were, relinquish it totally, and supplant it with the next, almost as if it were being done to you by an outside force over which you have no control. Strong emotions seize their victims.

The background to this scene is that Faulkland is engaged to

Julia: he saved her life when her boat overturned, and subsequently promised her father on his deathbed to marry her. His besetting sin is jealousy. He has just heard that Julia appeared in good spirits while separated from him, information which rendered him apoplectic. He is determined to have it out with her. She is all too familiar with his behaviour.

THE RIVALS

BY RICHARD BRINSLEY SHERIDAN

Act III, Scene 2

FAULKLAND: They told me Julia would return directly; I wonder she is not yet come! How mean does this captious, unsatisfied temper of mine appear to my cooler judgment! Yet I know not that I indulge it in any other point: but on this one subject, and to this one subject, whom I think I love beyond my life, I am ever ungenerously fretful, and madly capricious! I am conscious of it—yet I cannot correct myself! What tender, honest joy sparkled in her eyes when we met! How delicate was the warmth of her expressions! I was ashamed to appear less happy—though I had come resolved to wear a face of coolness and upbraiding. Sir Anthony's presence prevented my proposed expostulations—yet I must be satisfied that she has not been so very happy in my absence. She is coming! Yes! I know the nimbleness of her tread, when she thinks her impatient Faulkland counts the moments of her stay.

[*Enter* JULIA.]

JULIA: I had not hoped to see you again so soon.

FAULKLAND: Could I, Julia, be contented with my first welcome—restrained as we were by the presence of a third person?

JULIA: O Faulkland, when your kindness can make me thus happy, let me not think that I discovered something of coldness in your first salutation.

FAULKLAND: 'Twas but your fancy, Julia. I was rejoiced to see you—to see you in such health. Sure I had no cause for coldness?

JULIA: Nay then, I see you have taken something ill. You must not conceal from me what it is.

FAULKLAND: Well then—shall I own to you that my joy at hearing of your health and arrival here, by your neighbour Acres, was somewhat damped, by his dwelling much on the high spirits you had enjoyed in Devonshire—on your mirth—your singing—dancing, and I know not what! For such is my temper, Julia, that I should regard every mirthful moment in your absence as a treason to constancy. The mutual tear that steals down the cheek of parting lovers is a compact, that no smile shall live there till they meet again.

JULIA: Must I never cease to tax my Faulkland with this teasing minute caprice? Can the idle reports of a silly boor weigh in your breast against my tried affection?

FAULKLAND: They have no weight with me, Julia: no, no—I am happy if you have been so—yet only say, that you did not sing with *mirth*—say that you *thought* of Faulkland in the dance.

JULIA: I never can be happy, in your absence. If I wear a countenance of content, it is to show that my mind holds no doubt of my Faulkland's truth. If I seemed sad, it were to make malice triumph and say that I had fixed my heart on one who left me to lament his roving, and my own credulity. Believe me, Faulkland, I mean not to upbraid you, when I say, that I have often dressed sorrow in smiles, lest my friends should guess whose unkindness had caused my tears.

FAULKLAND: You were ever all goodness to me. O, I am a brute, when I but admit a doubt of your true constancy!

JULIA: If ever, without such cause from you, as I will not suppose possible, you find my affections veering but a point, may I become a proverbial scoff for levity, and base ingratitude.

FAULKLAND: Ah! Julia, that *last* word is grating to me. I would I had no title to your *gratitude*! Search your heart, Julia; perhaps what you have mistaken for Love, is but the warm effusion of a too thankful heart!

JULIA: For what quality must I love you?

FAULKLAND: For no quality! To regard me for any quality of mind or understanding, were only to *esteem* me. And for person—I have often wished myself deformed, to be convinced that I owed no obligation there for any part of your affection.

JULIA: Where Nature has bestowed a show of nice attention in the features of a man, he should laugh at it, as misplaced. I have seen men, who in this vain article perhaps might rank above you; but my heart has never asked my eyes if it were so or not.

FAULKLAND: Now this is not well from you, Julia—I despise

person in a man. Yet if you loved me as I wish, though there were an Aethiop, you'd think none so fair.

JULIA: I see you are determined to be unkind.—The contract which my poor father bound us in gives you more than a lover's privilege.

FAULKLAND: Again, Julia, you raise ideas that feed and justify my doubts. I would not have been more free—no—I am proud of my restraint. Yet—yet—perhaps your high respect alone for this solemn compact has fettered your inclinations, which else had made a worthier choice. How shall I be sure, had you remained unbound in thought and promise, that I should still have been the object of your persevering love?

JULIA: Then try me now. Let us be free as strangers as to what is past: my heart will not feel more liberty!

FAULKLAND: There now! so hasty, Julia! so anxious to be free! If your love for me were fixed and ardent, you would not lose your hold, even though I wished it!

JULIA: O, you torture me to the heart! I cannot bear it.

FAULKLAND: I do not mean to distress you. If I lov'd you less, I should never give you an uneasy moment. But hear me. All my fretful doubts arise from this—women are not used to weigh, and separate the motives of their affections: the cold dictates of prudence, gratitude, or filial duty, may sometimes be mistaken for the pleadings of the heart. I would not boast—yet let me say, that I have neither age, person, or character, to found dislike on; my fortune such as few ladies, could be charged with indiscretion in the match. O, Julia! when Love receives such countenance from *Prudence*, nice minds will be suspicious of its birth.

JULIA: I know not whither your insinuations would tend: But as they seem pressing to insult me—I will spare you the regret of having done so. I have given you no cause for this!

[*Exit in tears.*]

FAULKLAND: In tears! stay, Julia: stay but for a moment. The door is fastened! Julia—my soul—but for one moment—I hear her sobbing! 'Sdeath! What a brute I am to use her thus! Yet stay. Aye—she is coming now—how little resolution there is in woman—how a few soft words can turn them! No, faith—she is not coming either. Why, Julia—my love—say but that you forgive me—come but to tell me that—now this is being too resentful—stay! She is coming too—I thought she would—no steadiness in anything! Her going away must have been a mere trick then—she shan't see that I was hurt by it. I'll affect indifference— [*Hums a tune: then listens.*] No—Zounds! she's not coming! —nor don't intend it, I suppose. This is not steadiness but obstinacy! Yet I deserve it. What, after so long an absence, to quarrel with her tenderness—'twas barbarous and unmanly! —I should be ashamed to see her now. —I'll wait till her just resentment is abated—and when I distress her so again, may I lose her forever and be linked instead to some antique virago, whose gnawing passions, and long-hoarded spleen, shall make me curse my folly half the day, and all the night.

If you are playing Faulkland I suggest you use different colored marker pens to identify his changes of mood, because otherwise they are upon you and gone before you know it. Like any slalom racer you have to get to know the precise positions of the posts before you can race down the mountain. Some of the changes are a matter for debate. A lively way to test alternatives is to read the text with two or more actors: a different voice takes over for each change of mood. This has the useful side effect of causing the speaker to occupy the mood at the top of the sentence, to stake a claim to that mood, rather than slithering towards it during the course of the sentence. If tentativeness or lack of clarity remains, I have found that it can be productive to ask the actress playing Julia to try to leave the room whenever Faulkland offends her. Then, as Faulkland instinctively tries to hook her back with a change of tack, his attack and immediacy intensify to great effect.

You will notice that the language in this scene is sometimes rather florid, pompous even. This artificial literary diction is in the "sentimental" style popular in the eighteenth century, and the important thing here is that it is used selectively. Both Faulkland and Julia move in and out of this manner of speaking. They take their romance very, very seriously, and perceive it as an event requiring a grandeur of expression. The passionate linguistics only vanish when the characters are shocked into immediacy.

Like everything else on the page, this variation in their styles of speech is a clue for the actors. Working on a great text is a never-ending stimulus because there is always more to unearth and the interpretations are endlessly variable: in this analysis I can only show a tiny proportion of what can be extracted.

THE RIVALS
Act III, Scene 2
ANALYSIS

In the first speech, Faulkland is alone at Julia's lodgings, waiting for her to appear. He was profoundly dissatisfied with their last meeting. Who is he talking to—the audience or himself? It's always a problem to know who you are speaking to when you are alone on stage. There's no stage direction saying "Aside." Asides are a sort of hot-line to a sympathetic listener in the audience and they are always truthful. It's as if the actor leaves the time-scheme of the scene for a moment to reveal his innermost thoughts. In filmic terms it would be like looking directly at the camera before rejoining the action. But I don't think that's what's happening here. It seems to me that Faulkland is at a pitch of exasperation that would plausibly account for him talking to himself. It's as if you or I turned up for a doctor's appointment only to find the door locked. "But he *told* me to come at nine o'clock," we say, voicing our frustration whether anyone is there to listen or not. Having established his displeasure in the first sentence, Faulkland embarks on a psychiatric self-examination that sounds like a private session to me, and the sort of thing a self-obsessed fellow quite plausibly embarks on. It's entirely believable that this man should talk about himself to himself, for he is a supreme egoist. To share any uncertainty about his behavior with an audience implies a potential for guilt which would undercut the splendid and unexpected finale to the scene. By all means try the speech as an extended aside, but if you keep a detached perspective about its function in the scene, I think you will find it makes more sense as a monologue directed to himself.

FAULKLAND: **They told me Julia would return directly; I wonder she is not yet come! —How mean does this captious, unsatisfied temper of mine appear to my cooler judgment! Yet I know not that I indulge it in any other point: —but on this one subject, and to**

> this one subject, whom I think I love beyond my life, I am ever ungenerously fretful, and madly capricious! —I am conscious of it—yet I cannot correct myself! What tender, honest joy sparkled in her eyes when we met! —How delicate was the warmth of her expressions! —I was ashamed to appear less happy—though I had come resolved to wear a face of coolness and upbraiding. Sir Anthony's presence prevented my proposed expostulations: —yet I must be satisfied that she has not been so very happy in my absence. —She is coming! —Yes! —I know the nimbleness of her tread, when she thinks her impatient Faulkland counts the moments of her stay.

"Captious" means "finicky" or "nit-picking." Faulkland is saying how unpleasant his finicky, dissatisfied temperament seems to him when he is calmer. But how much more vivid and immediate this statement becomes if he isn't just referring to his previous encounter with Julia (which we didn't see) but to the previous *sentence*. So if he is extremely exasperated on his first line—and it does have an exclamation mark at the end of it—he can metaphorically clap his hand over his mouth on the second. It is his first swoop round the slalom pole in this scene and in paraphrase it would look like:

> "They *said* Julia would be here, where the **hell** is she— [*Slalom One*] —what a pig I can be when I'm jealous!"

Immediately the next pole looms. In Faulkland's case they are very often signalled by the word "yet." This is a less abrupt change of mood, but a change nevertheless.

> *Slalom Two*: "Yet I only behave in this crazy way to the one I love best. I'm aware of this but I don't seem to be able to do anything about it."

He is absolving himself of responsibility. He doesn't behave like this to anyone but Julia. The actor must decide whether Faulkland is genuinely puzzled by his own inability to reform, or whether he is implying that his behavior is partly Julia's fault.

I've said elsewhere that in high comedy there is only one moment and that moment is now, and there is a nostalgia hurdle to overcome in Faulkland's memory of Julia's appearance: "What tender honest joy sparkled in her eyes when we met! How delicate was the warmth of her expressions!" We don't want any colorless past-tense acting, and there's no justification for it, since the passage of a few hours wouldn't dim the power of that meeting, nor the importance of two points to a jealous man: "*Honest* joy"—what a reassurance—and unfeigned, "*delicate*" warmth. So although he's describing the past, his emotions are very much in the present.

Her welcome shamed him even though he had intended to show his disapproval of her reported behavior at the dance. Sir Anthony's presence also prevented his pouring out his displeasure. You'd think he might be grateful that these two events prevented him making a scene, but what does he say? "*Yet.*"

Slalom Three: "...yet I must be satisfied that she has not been so very happy in my absence."

End of rational thought, start of onslaught of jealousy. He must proceed with his investigation and reassure himself that Julia wasn't disloyal enough to be merry when her lover was away. Incidentally, it's worth noting that he says "so *very* happy"—implying that he is a reasonable man, that to be a little bit happy in his absence would be fine, but to be *very* happy is clearly beyond the pale.

The footsteps that herald her arrival knock him off his moralistic perch.

Slalom Four: The language is spontaneous, exclamatory:

"She is coming—yes!"

Then smugness sets in, and the tone changes and becomes more florid.

JULIA: I had not hoped to see you again so soon.

We have just learned from Faulkland that she greeted him with warmth and delight on the previous occasion. We also learned that he didn't behave impeccably—"I was ashamed to appear less happy"—so Julia must have observed the warning signals of jealousy with which she is so horribly familiar. But here we discover her to be an incorrigible optimist, for if she has any fears about this meeting she is determined to conceal them. As Faulkland complacently points out, she comes running to meet him. She has decided—as usual—to discount the possibility of danger and behave as if everything were perfect. Anyone who lives with an emotional time bomb is very wary of setting him (or her) off with implied criticism.

"I had not hoped to see you again so soon" may well have a subtext of "*why* are you here again so soon?" As we've discussed in connection with irony, the actress should acknowledge this possibility in rehearsal, but be aware that if it creeps through too strongly, Faulkland will spot it and react, possibly disastrously. It's a fine balance and perhaps could be most truthfully achieved through a really spontaneous delight at seeing him, followed by a slightly careful choice of words for her greeting.

> FAULKLAND: **Could I, Julia, be contented with my first welcome—restrained as we were by the presence of a third person?**

Do we believe that the presence of a third person is any sort of inhibition? I think we have the right to be extremely sceptical, since Faulkland behaved appallingly in the earlier scene with Jack Absolute and Bob Acres, giving way to his jealousy without the smallest attempt at control when he learned that Julia had sung and danced in his absence. However, even if it's not strictly true, it seems he manages to deliver the sentiment warmly enough for Julia to be sufficiently encouraged to offer a mild reproof:

> JULIA: **O Faulkland, when your kindness can make me thus happy, let me not think that I discovered something of coldness in your first salutation.**

> FAULKLAND: **'Twas but your fancy, Julia. I was rejoiced to see you—to see you in such health. Sure I had no cause for coldness?**

Faulkland is disabled by her perception: his speech becomes erratic and he answers with a question that immediately betrays his jealousy. (Maybe he can't bring himself to accuse her of happiness, that ultimate crime, so he substitutes another word beginning with "h" . . . ?) He's kept his cool for precisely one exchange.

> JULIA: **Nay then, I see you have taken something ill. —**
> **You must not conceal from me what it is.**

Is it fanciful to hear the tone of a hospital nurse in Julia's reply? It's one of those vistas into a previous life that I find so useful. She has been through all this before—oh God, here we go, let's sort it out as fast as possible.

> FAULKLAND: **Well then—shall I own to you that my joy**
> **at hearing of your health and arrival here, by your**
> **neighbour Acres, was somewhat damped, by his**
> **dwelling much on the high spirits you had enjoyed**
> **in Devonshire—on your mirth—your singing—**
> **dancing, and I know not what! For such is my tem-**
> **per, Julia, that I should regard every mirthful**
> **moment in your absence as a treason to constancy.**
> **The mutual tear that steals down the cheek of**
> **parting lovers is a compact, that no smile shall live**
> **there till they meet again.**

"Somewhat damped" is a wonderful understatement, for Faulkland's joy on hearing of her arrival in Bath was *annihilated* by Acre's casual mention of Julia's high spirits in Devonshire, and he made a complete and utter exhibition of himself. It's like someone who has started a brawl in a pub, destroyed the furniture, and been sick over the landlord saying, "Had a spot of trouble." Is that list of her sins—mirth, singing, dancing—in escalating order of culpability? Just when we think that dreadful litany is going to set him off again, he gains control of himself by his usual means—pomposity. The last two sentences are the acme of the "sentimental" style.

> JULIA: **Must I never cease to tax my Faulkland with this**

**teasing minute caprice? Can the idle reports of a
silly boor weigh in your breast against my tried affection?**

Julia, in my opinion, deserves a post at a major psychiatric hospital. Presumably she makes two attempts at soothing his savage
breast simply because he doesn't respond to the first. They are
both brilliant—the reassurance of "*my* Faulkland" and "my *tried*
affection." And—possibly fed up by the fact she has to make the
second effort—she manages a subtle reproach, with that "tried."

FAULKLAND: **They have no weight with me, Julia: no,
no —I am happy if you have been so—yet only say,
that you did not sing with mirth—say that you
thought of Faulkland in the dance.**

Since Faulkland has already admitted his caprice to himself, he can
only respond reasonably, but even by the time he gets to the repe-
tition of the "no"—always a giveaway, why say it twice? —his jealousy has usurped his sense. And a real sign of desperation is that he
lowers his expectation of her behaviour: "*only* say you did not sing
with mirth—say you *thought* of Faulkland in the dance." Suddenly
the singing and dancing are not by themselves evidence of betrayal!

JULIA: **I never can be happy in your absence. If I wear
a countenance of content, it is to show that my
mind holds no doubt of my Faulkland's truth. If I
seemed sad, it were to make malice triumph and
say that I had fixed my heart on one who left me
to lament his roving, and my own credulity.
Believe me, Faulkland, I mean not to upbraid you,
when I say that I have often dressed sorrow in
smiles, lest my friends should guess whose unkindness had caused my tears.**

Now it is Julia's turn to come up a notch, stylistically. The re-
peated "if" gives the speech the quality of an aria. Like an aria, the
home truths build to a crescendo—they get tougher and tougher.

She is taking a risk of upsetting him, even with the caveat of "I mean not to upbraid you," but it appears to pay off:

> FAULKLAND: **You were ever all goodness to me. O, I am a brute, when I but admit a doubt of your true constancy!**

Faulkland flings himself round the slalom pole in an agony of self-abasement. The intensity must surpass all the previous manifestations of jealousy in the scene, because it spurs Julia into the mistake of not leaving well enough alone but launching into another assurance:

> JULIA: **If ever, without such cause from you, as I will not suppose possible, you find my affections veering but a point, may I become a proverbial scoff for levity, and base ingratitude.**

Note the positivity of the consonants in the last line; it's strong stuff and *ought* to be utterly reassuring.

> FAULKLAND: **Ah! Julia, that last word is grating to me. I would I had no title to your gratitude! Search your heart, Julia; perhaps what you have mistaken for Love, is but the warm effusion of a too thankful heart!**

He slaloms into the attack, pouncing on the word "gratitude." It's not a sufficiently noble emotion to be associated with their love, capital L. He adopts a maddeningly evangelical tone.

> JULIA: **For what quality must I love you?**
>
> FAULKLAND: **For no quality! To regard me for any quality of mind or understanding, were only to esteem me. And for person—I have often wish'd myself deformed, to be convinced that I owed no obligation there for any part of your affection.**

Julia asks a despairing question, only to have her vocabulary derided and her intentions proclaimed unworthy. Only the loftiest language and emotions are appropriate for their love, declares Faulkland, sustaining his recently achieved position of piety and wincing at "quality," "gratitude," and "esteem" as though he had found blasphemies in a hymn. What a marvellous unintentional revelation of vanity is contained in his wish to be deformed!

> JULIA: **Where Nature has bestowed a show of nice attention in the features of a man, he should laugh at it, as misplaced. I have seen men, who in this vain article perhaps might rank above you; but my heart has never asked my eyes if it were so or not.**

Julia is no wimp and she goes into battle with a double broadside, tempered with her usual prudence:

1. "Goodlooking men should discount their looks."

2. "I've seen plenty of men who *perhaps*" (she's not too cross to take the elementary precaution of "perhaps") "were better looking than you."

And hastens to add another anti-jealousy precaution, "But I've never bothered to look with any real interest."

> FAULKLAND: **Now this is not well from you, Julia—I despise person in a man. Yet if you loved me as I wish, though I were an Aethiop, you'd think none so fair.**

Faulkland maintains his censorious tone, reiterating his own wonderful lack of vanity ("person" means good looks), and with staggering illogicality accuses her of not loving him enough.

> JULIA: **I see you are determined to be unkind. The contract which my poor father bound us in gives you more than a lover's privilege.**

This is remakably direct stuff for Julia. It seems that the provocation has hit home. The "contract" is, of course, Faulkland's assurance to Julia's late father that he would marry her daughter. He's behaving as badly as a husband.

FAULKLAND: **Again, Julia, you raise ideas that feed and justify my doubts. I would not have been more free—no—I am proud of my restraint. Yet—yet— perhaps your high respect alone for this solemn compact has fettered your inclinations, which else had made a worthier choice. How shall I be sure, had you remained unbound in thought and promise, that I should still have been the object of your persevering love?**

To me, Faulkland has assumed something of the mantle of the prosecuting counsel in his last few speeches, by employing phrases like "search your heart" and "now this is not well." Now he is employing more orator's tricks such as, "Again, Julia"; the reinforcing "no," and the "yet—yet" that falsely implies measured consideration. He pounds out his message with increasing fervour—it's pure demagoguery, brimming with moral loftiness.

JULIA: **Then try me now. Let us be free as strangers as to what is past—my heart will not feel more liberty!**

This is more defiant still; her language gets simpler as he hurts her more.

FAULKLAND: **There now! so hasty, Julia! so anxious to be free! If your love for me were fixed and ardent, you would not lose your hold, even though I wished it!**

He's like a lawyer seizing joyfully on his adversary's slip-up: "There now!" Despite his legal-eagle mannerisms, he's out of control; his logic is contemptible.

JULIA: **O, you torture me to the heart! —I cannot bear it.**

Julia is now completely stripped of all artifice: this is a cry from the heart.

FAULKLAND: **I do not mean to distress you. If I loved you less, I should never give you an uneasy moment. But hear me. All my fretful doubts arise from this—**

women are not used to weigh, and separate the motives of their affections—the cold dictates of prudence, gratitude, or filial duty, may sometimes be mistaken for the pleadings of the heart. I would not boast—yet let me say, that I have neither age, person, or character, to found dislike on; my fortune such as few ladies, could be charged with indiscretion in the match. O, Julia! when love receives such countenance from prudence, nice minds will be suspicious of its birth.

"I do not mean to distress you" could be a stiff unfeeling apology, or it could be a swift slalom into a repentant swain. Either way he reverts to self-justification (and, incidentally, a vista of his concept of love). Then he is back into lecturing mode, having established his superiority as an analyst of relationships. We know Julia to be a thoughtful, serious girl, and Faulkland pitches his criticisms as if they were of women in general, rather than her in particular. But while he is ostensibly attacking womankind, it's obvious that he is really blaming *her*, because he uses all the words and issues that have been a source of conflict between them in the scene. "Prudence," "gratitude," and "filial duty" are all specific javelin thrusts at Julia. You will make sense of his boast about his fortune if you slightly emphasise the word "such"—here it means "so much" or "so great." He's rich enough to be a good match. Although he started off with a lofty judiciousness, his oratory gets the better of him, as usual. "O Julia !" is a dramatic accusation. But what is the charge? That if their great romantic love has any streak of caution in it, people of refined sensibility—"nice minds" (like Faulkland's)—will not consider it to be love at all. "Prudence, gratitude and filial duty" are *her* inappropriate contributions to passion—he drives her from the room with his condescension.

JULIA: **I know not whither your insinuations would tend: But as they seem pressing to insult me, I will spare you the regret of having done so. I have given you no cause for this! [*Exit in tears.*]**

Within the scene so far, the balance of power has shifted several times, but since the first use of that dread word "gratitude;" Faulkland has been on, if not a winning, at least a bullying streak. From the same point onwards, Julia has progressively become less affected in her speech patterns, Faulkland more.

When the ultimate reality of her tears, her exit, and the door slam finally penetrate his bluster, all traces of "sentimentality" leave him and he embarks on the slalom course to end all slalom courses, concluding with a poetic and passionate invocation.

FAULKLAND: **In tears! stay, Julia: stay but for a moment.—** SLALOM—The door is fastened! —SLALOM— Julia—my soul—but for one moment—SLALOM—I hear her sobbing! —SLALOM—'Sdeath! what a brute I am to use her thus! —SLALOM—Yet stay.— SLALOM—Aye—she is coming now: how little resolution there is in woman! How a few soft words can turn them! —SLALOM—No, faith! —she is not coming either.—SLALOM—Why, Julia—my love—say but that you forgive me—come but to tell me that— SLALOM—now this is being too resentful— SLALOM—stay! she is coming too—SLALOM—I thought she would—no steadiness in anything! — SLALOM—Her going away must have been a mere trick then—she shan't see that I was hurt by it. I'll affect indifference—[*Hums a tune: then listens.*]— SLALOM—No, Zounds! she's not coming! —nor don't intend it, I suppose. This is not steadiness but obstinacy! —SLALOM—Yet I deserve it. What, after so long an absence, to quarrel with her tenderness! 'Twas barbarous and unmanly! —SLALOM—I should be ashamed to see her now. I'll wait till her just resentment is abated—SLALOM—and when I distress her so again, may I lose her forever, and be linked instead to some antique virago, whose gnaw-

**ing passions, and long-hoarded spleen, shall make
me curse folly half the day, and all the night.**

The slalom course having been identified (there are alternative readings, naturally), then comes the business of finding the right level of
emotion. It is far higher than most actors think. Identify each separate emotional state; paraphrase it into contemporary English if you
cannot find the right inflection; then repeat it three times in the
original words, escalating the fervor each time. It's not a question of
volume, it's a question of intensity. You will go further than you
thought possible without sacrificing reality, and you will probably
still only be scaling the foothills of Faulkland's astonishing volatility.

Actresses often ask me for a female equivalent of this dizzying
exercise. *The Double Dealer*, by William Congreve, has a glorious
scene which makes demands similar to the Faulkland scenes in *The
Rivals*. I have marked some of the most obvious potential slalom
poles in the extract which follows (\), but there are many other potential choices. In the plot to this point, we have learned that
young Mellefont loves young Cynthia. However, her vain, un-
principled stepmother, Lady Plyant, believes she herself is the se-
cret object of his affections, and that the romance with Cynthia is
a cover-up. The verbal contortions which follow consist of Lady
Plyant's ill-concealed lust for Mellefont alternating with attempts
at respectability. The flashes of demureness are themselves part of
her arsenal of flirtation: they are *paraded* before the stupified man.
She recoils from sins of the flesh while simultaneously managing
to suggest they are lip-smackingly delightful. The great difference
between this and the Faulkland scene is that Lady Plyant is completely aware of what she is doing: her slalom is a grotesque
courtship dance, intended to fascinate.

THE DOUBLE DEALER

BY WILLIAM CONGREVE

Act II, Scene 1

LADY PLYANT: O, such a thing! The impiety of it startles me! To wrong so good, so fair a creature, and one that loves you tenderly; 'tis a barbarity of barbarities, and nothing could be guilty of it—

MELLEFONT: —but the greatest villain imagination can form. I grant it; and next to the villainy of such a fact is the villainy of aspersing me with such a guilt. How? which way was I to wrong her? for yet I understand you not.

LADY PLYANT: Why, gad's my life, cousin Mellefont, you cannot be so peremptory as to deny it, when I tax you with it to your face!

MELLEFONT: By heaven, I love her more than life, or—

LADY PLYANT: \ Fiddle, faddle, don't tell me of this or that, and everything in the world, but give me mathemacular demonstration, answer me directly— \ But I have not the patience \ —Oh, the impiety of it ! as I was saying, and the unparalleled wickedness! O merciful Father! how could you think to reverse nature so—to make the daughter the means of procuring the mother?

MELLEFONT: The daughter to procure the mother!

LADY PLYANT: Ay, for though I am not Cynthia's own mother, I am her father's wife, and that's near enough to make it incest.

MELLEFONT: [*Aside.*] Incest! O my precious aunt and the devil in conjunctiom!

LADY PLYANT: O reflect upon the horror of that, and the guilt of deceiving everybody; marrying the daughter only to make a cuckold of the father; and then \ seducing me, debauching my purity and perverting me from the road of virtue \ in which I have trod thus long, and never made one trip, not one *faux pas*; O consider it, what would you have to answer for, if you should provoke me to frailty? \ Alas! humanity is feeble, heaven knows! very feeble and unable to support itself.

MELLEFONT: Where am I? is it day? and am I awake? Madam—

LADY PLYANT: And nobody knows how circumstances may happen together— \ To my thinking now, I could resist the strongest temptation— \ But yet I know 'tis impossible for me to know whether I could or not; there's no certainty in the things of this life.

MELLEFONT: Madam, pray give me leave to ask you one question.

LADY PLYANT: \ O lord, ask me the question! \ I'll swear I'll refuse it! I swear I'll deny it! \ —therefore don't ask me; \ nay, you shan't ask me; \ I swear I'll deny it. \ O gemini, you have brought all the blood into my face! I warrant I am as red as a turkey-cock; O fie, cousin Mellefont!

MELLEFONT: Nay, madam, hear me; I mean—

LADY PLYANT: \ Hear you! no, no; \ I'll deny you first and hear you afterward. \ For one does not know how one's mind may change upon hearing. Hearing is one of the senses, and all the senses are fallible; I won't trust my honour, I assure you; \ my honour is infallible—

MELLEFONT: For heaven's sake, madam—

LADY PLYANT: O name it no more! Bless me, how can you talk of heaven! and have so much wickedness in your heart? \

Maybe you don't think it a sin. They say some of you gentlemen don't think it a sin. Maybe it is no sin to them that don't think it so; indeed, if I did not think it a sin— \ but still my honour, if it were no sin. \ But then to marry my daughter for the conveniency of frequent opportunities, I'll never consent to that; as sure as can be, I'll break the match.

MELLEFONT: Death and amazement! Madam, upon my knees—

LADY PLYANT: \ Nay, nay rise up! come, you shall see my good nature. I know love is powerful, and nobody can help his passion: 'tis not your fault, nor I swear it is not mine. How can I help it if I have charms? and how can you help it if you are made a captive? I swear it is pity it should be a fault. \ But my honour— \ well, but your honour too— \ but the sin! \ well, but the necessity— \ O lord, here's somebody coming, I dare not stay. \ Well, you must consider of your crime; an strive as much as can be against it- strive, be sure— \ but don't be melancholic, don't despair. \ But never think that I'll grant you anything; O Lord, no. \ But be sure you lay aside all thoughts of the marriage: for though I know you don't love Cynthia, only as a blind to your passion for me, yet it will make me jealous. \ O Lord, what did I say? jealous! no, no, I can't be jealous, for I must not love you— \ therefore don't hope— \ but don't despair neither. \ O, they're coming! I must fly. [*Exit.*]

6

WHAT IS STYLE?

Style is not a manner of performing. It is the relationship between content and form. The content includes the society of the play, the genre of the play, and the period both of play and author. The form is the manner in which we express these characteristics. There are, unfortunately, no short cuts to discovering this relationship.

Every play, even if written this year, is a time capsule, containing elements representative of its own particular culture—in other words, it has a style which is not an affectation, which is decipherable through its content, and which is not something grafted onto it. When Sir John Gielgud said, "Style is knowing what sort of play you're in," he made a deceptively simple statement. If we can find out precisely what is unique, what is *particular*, what differentiates the world of this play from all others, then we discover its style.

Style must avoid cliché: it has to be based on the creation of a world. If it's second-hand then we've failed to make the playwright's vision real. (Real doesn't preclude surreal or historical or fantastic—it just means that the world of the play has its own logic which the participants experience first-hand, so it is real for them.) We can't achieve style unless we make this attempt to create a new reality, for "reality" is a fresh concept new-minted by a particular playwright for each particular play. Charles Lamb, writing about Congreve's plays, said, "I could never connect those sports of a witty fancy...to an imitation of real life. They are a world of themselves almost as much as fairyland." He perceives that because the plays do not imitate life, this in no way denies them a reality *of their own*. It's fatal for actors to begin with the premise that they are involved in an unreal world. We create a new world every time we do a play.

Creating a world is the first step in finding the style of a play. How do we do this? We find the life that comprises such a world first by detective work on the text and second by the use of the collaborative "if." The first phase requires us to ask the right questions of a text; then, using only available facts, to calculate what is normal in the society of the play. The second phase requires us to agree on our interpretation of the unavailable facts. These add up to a society unique to this piece of work. Recognition of the rules of the world in which you function is the fundamental prerequisite of style.

Having understood that style is not a frill but a necessity for everyone in the play, you must collaborate in the acknowledgment and possible creation of its rules. For in order to survive in any given world, you have to obey its rules or face the consequences. If you appear in a court of law, you adopt its specialized decorum. If you join a cricket team, your conduct in the pavilion would differ from a footballer's behavior in the changing room. Think how one adapts to a country's style simply in order to get what one wants; how different the whole breakfast culture is in the U.S. from that of Europe or the U.K., and the confusion one would cause by asking for eggs "over easy" in Britain. Style isn't something invented by the theatre; it's fundamental to our survival. If you adopt a certain way of behaving you do not perceive it as an affectation (although others may), but simply as a means of getting what you want.

All discoveries have to be made through your character. Where else could you begin? You can't play style in the abstract, you can only play it insofar as it is manifested by your character; your character's attributes rubbing up against environment, period, social values. Hard textual and contextual evidence and socio-historical research are indispensable, but the greatest gift an actor brings to the problem of style is his imagination. Because when we bring the gift of imagination to our work, we create truth simply by believing. Onstage whatever the actors believe in is true! "The *feeling of truth*," a phrase coined by Stanislavsky, is what distinguishes powerful magic from whimsy in productions of fantasy such as *The Tempest* or *A Midsummer Night's Dream*. If the actors have made a living texture and a working logic in the kingdoms of Prospero or Oberon, then those worlds become palpable realities for the audience too.

You will be taking possession of another time—could be the seventeenth century, could be last year. Twentieth-century perspective is often irrelevant; try not to see everything through the prism of modern opinion, or through your own culture. A knowledge of the tastes and preferences which belong to each period are vital to the interpretation of a play. It doesn't matter if your director puts you all into pink spacesuits in his production of *The Way Of The World*, he can't alter the mores of the characters who people it. You have to play them, and you must understand what motivates them in their world, which necessitates an understanding of their times. Your director can't tamper with the fact that in the Restoration adultery was acceptable, but sex before marriage was not, for example—the play turns on that fulcrum. The purpose of a formula like "Restoration comedy" is to define limits beyond which certain judgements are arbitrary and anachronistic. If you are cast in a Victorian play, you must discover that Victorian culture valued women who were reticent, emotionally sensitive, monogamously loyal, languid, fastidious in sensibility, frugal, and capable of histrionics. How many of these qualities are rewarded today? A modern stance will bring us no nearer to discovering the essence of such a heroine. In current American society, the bereaved are offered anti-depressants if grief persists into a second year. In rural Greek society, a widow is expected to mourn for five years; less would be shocking and disrespectful. In the pursuit of the style of the play we must reconstruct our culture from the ground up. What are the differences between our world and the world of the play that make the play *itself*?

In his excellent book *Acting Power*, Robert Cohen offers the best practical help that I have come across for analyzing the world of a play. He suggests that characterization is a mirror image of style: "Characterization is a measure of how the individual character differs from the other characters, and style is a measure of how much he resembles them." In order to establish those majority characteristics that comprise a world, Cohen suggests we analyze the text in terms of two basic questions: 1. What kind of behavior gets rewarded? 2. What kind of behavior gets punished? The answers create a a social backdrop against which everything is played out. All your character's expectations are conditioned by his knowledge of the answers to these questions. He is part of the "world" which they reveal. This doesn't blur the objectives you may have as a character, it simply places you in a context. Whether the character you are playing subscribes to these ideas or not, he or she must know and understand them. For example, if you live in a society with a passion for opera, a passion which you do not share, then you know you will constantly have to justify this oddity, or lie about it, or fight a losing battle trying to convert the world to your point of view. Style is a necessary element of performance, one that adds power and credibility to character, because it reveals character as not only a creation in itself but as part of a greater creation.

Robert Cohen has compiled an indispensible check list of questions to help us analyze a new world, and I have incorporated a few more that apply to high comedies; you will come up with others appropriate to your play. Some of the answers are in the text, some are established by research into the period, some you may invent in the absence of information. What is important is that the company agree with the conclusions. Style is only style if it is a shared set of ideas. Try asking the following of the characters in a play you know well:

✧ What kind of behavior gets rewarded?

✧ What kind of behavior gets punished?

✧ What draws their attention?

✧ What makes them respect someone?

✧ How do they respond to attempts at seduction?

✧ What puts them down?

✧ How frightened are they of physical force?

✧ What is sexy?

✧ What turns them off?

✧ What frightens them?

✧ How do they react when frightened?

✧ Do they have a sense of humour?

✧ What is fun to them?

✧ Do they like to have fun? To be seen having fun?

✧ What do they like in people?

✧ What makes them trust people?

✧ Do they treat their friends well?

✧ Do they fear eloquence?

✧ Do they admire it?

✧ What is their span of verbal attention?

✧ What kinds of words do they use?

✧ What kinds of syntax?

✧ What makes someone socially acceptable?

✧ What is fashionable?

✧ What would you be saying/wearing/doing to be fashionable?

✧ What is old-fashioned?

✧ What is their apparent moral code?

✧ What is their real moral code?

✧ What is rude?

✧ What is polite?

✧ What would constitute a scandal?

By finding out what motivates the majority and how their ambitions are made manifest, you gain a sense of how your character *ought* to be functioning, a sense of propriety in this particular world. This brings in its wake the essential ingredient of high comedy, the ability to recognize the incongruity and comic potential of impropriety. But, *pace* Robert Cohen, it only partially solves the question of style.

The next layer of style demands understanding and acknowledgment of the author's attitude to the subject. To put it crudely, you may be a baddie in the society of the play, but a goodie in the eyes of the playwright. Most heroes and heroines of high comedy are glamorous mavericks and thorns in the social flesh, and this aspect of the genre is in itself part of the style. So the style of a high comedy is established not only by discovering what the conventions that Beatrice in *Much Ado*, for example, or Millamant in *The Way Of The World*, or Amanda in *Private Lives*, are rebelling against, precisely, but also by making it clear that their choices are the ones the audience will share, at least for the duration of the play, *because that's the way the playwright's fixed it.*

Perhaps the most sophisticated requirement of style is that you partake of the essential mood of the play—an immersion that goes beyond characterization. Someone once said that the difference between acting in tragedy and acting in comedy is that in tragedy you begin the evening knowing that you're going to die. Well, in comedy you know you are going to end with something nice happening. It isn't just a question of genre recognition. To be in the style of the piece we must carry the possibility of the ending very deep inside us—in our character's subconscious, if you like—right from the beginning. We subscribe to impossible or unlikely events (think of the maelstrom of improbabilities in *The Importance*) just to have a happy ending; if we are really in the style, our spirits overpower our logic and *demand* one. Think of the end of *As You Like It*, riddled with absurd events. All that matters is that everyone gets paired off, satisfactorily or not. In *The Rivals* Julia is told, "There, marry him directly, you'll find he'll mend surprisingly." What possible evidence is there to make that breathtaking assumption about Faulkland? We must give up rationalization and go with the spirit—the style—of the play. It's a mindset that the actor owes the playwright. If you have difficulty in reconciling this with being in character, then lodge the predetermined pattern in his or her subconscious. Your understanding of the writer's intentions, the nature of the play, and its outcome can be so deep that it's like the aborigine's dream of his origins. However you do it, you must relish the cascade of unlikely events and give in to happy endings.

Noel Coward's plays can be easily sabotaged by a misunderstanding of their style. Most of them depend upon the collision of two sets of values: in *Hay Fever*, the conventional attitudes of the houseguests versus the unconventional ones of the Bliss family; in *Private Lives*, the cautious respectable middle-class virtues of Victor and Sybil versus the irresponsible hedonism of Elyot and Amanda; in *Design for Living*, the commercial ethos of art dealers and theatre producers versus the bohemian values of Leo, Otto and Gilda; in *The Vortex*, a forceful amorality versus a weaker morality. In each case, the second, rebellious group could not fully exist without the first: their behavior is a conscious act of defiance of convention. There would be no drama in the Bliss family's eccentricities if there was no-one to be bewildered by them. Amanda and Elyot must have conventional spouses to outrage and betray. Leo and Otto and Gilda find out what they really want—art and each other—by resisting commercial and conventional values. In *The Vortex*, Nicky nearly escapes his mother's ghastly world, but he is only a temporary tenant of that second, dissenting group and the play ends bleakly with little hope for him or Florence. This play is, in fact, a supreme example of the need to "know what sort of play you're in." You must carry the pessimistic ending with you from the beginning, just as with improbable happy endings. Not in such a way that you give off superficial signals about the nature of the play, but in the awareness that the comedy at the beginning must connect authentically with the ugly ending. The alternatives are that the first act appears to be a jolly curtain-raiser that's been grafted on, or that the last act is gratuitously melodramatic. Either way the style is lost. Style is, then, a distillation of attitudes which reflect the meaning of the play. Nemirovich-Danchenko, one of drama's greatest teachers and an important contributor to the Stanislavsky tradition, said that Stanislavsky always sought "the essence of the play in times and events described; and this he expected the actor to understand. This is what Stanislavsky called the core, and it is this core which must stir the actor, which must become part of him for the time being." Whether we call it the core, or the truth, or the style, what we mean is the play's *own* reality, which springs from its unique insights and values. If we can distil these things from a playwright's text, then we will perhaps have found the essence, the *style* of the play.

SELECTED
BIBLIOGRAPHY

Bergson, Henri. *Laughter*. Macmillan, New York 1913.

Callow, Simon. *Being an Actor*. Methuen London Ltd. 1984.

Cohen, Robert. *Acting Power*. Mayfield Publishing Company. 1978.

Cole, Toby and Helen Chinoy, Helen, Ed. *Actors on Acting*. Crown. New York 1970.

Hagen, Uta. *A Challenge for the Actor*. Macmillan. New York 1991.

Hagen, Uta. *Respect For Acting*. Macmillan. New York 1973.

Kronenberger, Louis. *The Thread of Laughter*. Knopf. New York 1952.

Redgrave, Michael. *The Actor's Ways and Means*. Theatre Arts Books. New York 1954.

Richards, Sandra. *The Rise of the English Actress*. Macmillan. London 1993.

Saint-Denis, Michel. *The Rediscovery of Style*. Theatre Arts Books. New York 1986.

Seyler, Athene and Haggard, Stephen. *The Craft of Comedy*. Nick Hern Books. London 1990.

Stone, Lawrence. *The Family, Sex and Marriage in England 91500-1800*. Harper and Row. New York 1979.

Styan, J. L. *The Dark Comedy*. Cambridge University Press. New York 1962

Styan, J. L. *Restoration Comedy in Performance*. Cambridge University Press 1986.

Maria Aitken's theatre credits include leading roles at the Royal National Theatre in *Blithe Spirit* (Coward) and *Bedroom Farce* (Ayckbourn); at the Royal Shakespeare Company in *Travesties* (Stoppard) and *Waste* (Granville Barker); and on the West End in *A Little Night Music* (Sondheim), *Other People's Money* (Sterner), *Sister Mary Ignatius Explains It All For You* (Durang), and *Private Lives, Design for Living, The Vortex,* and *Hay Fever* (Coward). She has played more Coward heroines in London than Gertrude Lawrence.

As director, her productions in the West End include *Happy Family* (Cooper) and *The Mystery of Irma Vep* (Ludlum), as well as *After the Ball* (Douglas Home) at the Old Vic and *As You Like It* in Regent's Park.

Among her many television appearances, she has co-starred in the sitcom "Poor Little Rich Girls"; has had two runs of her own chat show, "Private Lives"; and starred in the recent BBC series "Love on a Branch Line." Her film perfomances include *A Fish Called Wanda*, for which she was nominated for a BAFTA award, and John Cleese's film *Fierce Creatures*.

She is on the artistic board of Shakespeare's Globe Theatre and the International Foundation for Training in the Arts, and enjoys a long association with the Julliard School and the Yale School of Drama as a visiting professor when her acting schedule permits.

Ms. Aitken has an M.A. in English Literature from Oxford. She lives in New York and London with her husband, the novelist Patrick McGrath, and her son, actor Jack Davenport.

MARIA AITKEN

ACTING IN HIGH COMEDY

The 60 Minute BBC Master Class

"A LIVELY SESSION ON HIGH COMEDY, with examples from Coware, Wilde, Sheridan and Congreve ...(revealing) the spark that transforms a routine reading into a vibrant one in a scene from Private Lives which by the time Aitken has finished with it has attained SOMETHING CLOSE TO BRILLIANCE. "

—LONDON TIMES

"'Language is a kind of decoy for your real feelings' says MARIA AITKEN, A MAGICAL STYLIST OF HIGH COMEDY. In getting her young audience to play scenes fron Coward, Wilde and Restoration plays, she shows them and us exactly what she means. ENCHANTING!"

—DAILY MAIL

"MARIA AITKEN'S CLEAR THINK, LOGIC AND NATURAL GOOD TASTE MAKE HER ANALYSIS OF HIGH COMEDY A DELIGHT."

—THE MAIL ON SUNDAY

VIDEO: $39.95 • ISBN: 1-55783-116-5

❤APPLAUSE❤

ACTING IN
RESTORATION COMEDY

Based on the BBC Master Class Series
By Simon Callow

The art of acting in Restoration Comedy, the
buoyant, often bawdy romps which celebrated the
reopening of the English theatres after Cromwell's
dour reign, is the subject of Simon Callow's bold new
investigation. There is cause again to celebrate as
Callow, one of Britain's foremost actors, aims to
restore the form to all its original voluptuous vigor.
Callow shows the way to attain clarity and hilarity in
some of the most delightful roles ever conceived for
the theatre.

Simon Callow is the author of *Being an Actor* and
Charles Laughton: A Difficult Actor. He has won
critical acclaim for his performances in numerous
productions including *Faust, The Relapse,* and *Titus
Andronicus.*

paper • ISBN: 1-55783-119-X

STANISLAVSKI REVEALED
by Sonia Moore

Other than Stanislavski's own published work, the most widely read interpretation of his techniques remains Sonia Moore's pioneering study, The Stanislavski System. Sonia Moore is on the frontier again now as she reveals the subtle tissue of ideas behind what Stanislavski regarded as his "major breakthrough," the Method of Physical Actions. Moore has devoted the last decade in her world-famous studio to an investigation of Stanislavski's final technique. The result is the first detailed discussion of Moore's own theory of psychophysical unity which she has based on her intensive practical meditation on Stanislavski's consummate conclusions about acting.

Demolishing the popular notion that his methods depend on private—self-centered—expression, Moore now reveals Stanislavski as the advocate of deliberate, controlled, conscious technique—internal and external at the same time—a technique that makes tremendous demands on actors but that rewards them with the priceless gift of creative life.

paper • ISBN: 1-55783-103-3

SPEAK WITH DISTINCTION
by Edith Skinner

"Speak With Distinction is the **most comprehensive and accessible speech book available** for teachers and students of speech."
>—Joan Washington, RSC, Royal Court & Royal National Theatre

"Edith Skinner's book is the **best book on speech I have ever encountered**. It was my primer in school and it is my reference book now. To the classical actor, or for that matter any actor who wishes to be understood, this method is a sure guide."
>—Kevin Kline

"Speak with Distinction is **the single most important work on the actor's craft** of stage speech. Edith Skinner's work must be an indispensable source book for all who aspire to act."
>—Earle Gister, Yale School of Drama

paper•ISBN 1-155783-047-9

CREATING A CHARACTER:
A Physical Approach to Acting

by Moni Yakim with Muriel Broadman

"Moni Yakim's techniques to attain characterization have been outstandingly successful in bringing out of his students emotional depth to enrich whatever they do on stage. [He] is an inspired teacher. His ideas and practices, which the book details, make it required reading for every serious student of the theatre."
—from the foreword by Stella Adler

"So often actors forget that there are bodies attached to their character's heads. Through Moni Yakim's technique I learned to develop the physical life of a character, lifting the character off the page and into reality."

—Patti Lupone

"Moni Yakim's teaching awakens the actor's senses and tunes the actor's physicality to a degree of self-expression beyond the merely naturalistic and into the larger realms of imagination and poetry."

—Kevin Kline

paper • ISBN: 1-55783-161-0

MICHAEL CHEKHOV:
ON THEATER AND THE ART OF ACTING
The Six Hour Master Class
Four 90-minute Audio Cassettes
by Michael Chekhov

edited with a 48-page course guide
by Mala Powers

AN AUDIO TREASURE!

Join the legendary teacher/director, heralded as Russia's greatest actor, for a six hour master class on the fundamentals of the Chekhov technique. Among the features:

- The Art of Characterization
- Short Cuts to Role Preparation
- How to Awaken Artistic Feelings and Emotions
- Avoiding Monotony in Performance
- Overcoming Inhibitions and Building Self-Confidence
- Psycho-physical Exercises
- Development of the Ensemble Spirit

$49.95 X
ISBN: 1-55783-117-3

MICHAEL CAINE
ACTING IN FILM
An Actor's Take on Movie Making

Academy Award winning actor Michael Caine, internationally acclaimed for his talented performances in movies for over 25 years, reveals secrets for success on screen. *Acting in Film* is also available on video (the BBC Master Class).

"Michael Caine knows the territory...*Acting in Film* is wonderful reading, even for those who would not dream of playing 'Lets Pretend' in front of a camera. Caine's guidance, aimed at novices still dreaming of the big break, can also give hardened critics fresh insights to what it is they're seeing up there on the screen..."
   –Charles Champlin, LOS ANGELES TIMES

BOOK/PAPER: $10.95• ISBN: 1-55783-124-6
BOOK/CLOTH: $14.95 • ISBN: 0-936839-86-4
VIDEO: $29.95 • ISBN: 1-55783-034-7

JANET SUZMAN

ACTING IN SHAKESPEAREAN COMEDY

The 60 Minute BBC Master Class

"Suzman is a major classical actress... she is also a born teacher ... beneath her flame-colored hair, Suzman burned and her students duly caught fire ... she persistently came out with striking stimulating remarks (with) workshop snippets of *Much Ado, As You Like It* and *Twelfth Night."*
—Benedict Nightingale, LONDON TIMES

"Totally and incisively in charge, her unscripted preamble is a dramatic lesson in itself, with all the right places to create dramatic effect you can cut with a knife. Her dissertation on the difference between tragedy and comedy is masterly."
—Sunday Times (London)

Janet Suzman is well-known for her may theatrical, film and television appearances. She is an Honorary Associate Artist of the Royal Shakespeare Company where her work over the years has included THE COMEDY OF ERRORS, THE MERCHANT OF VENICE, and ANTONY & CLEOPATRA

VIDEO: $39.95 • ISBN: 1-55783-115-7
Also in book form: Paper • $12.95 • ISBN: 1-55783-215-3